A Handbook for

CLINICAL and ACTUARIAL MMPI INTERPRETATION

HAROLD GILBERSTADT, Ph.D.

Chief Clinical Psychologist, Minneapolis VA
Hospital and Associate Professor,
Division of Clinical Psychology,
University of Minnesota Medical School

JAN DUKER, Ph.D.

Associate Professor of Psychology, Educational
Psychology and Child Development and Director
of School Psychology Training Program,
University of Minnesota

UNIVERSITY
PRESS OF
AMERICA

LANHAM • NEW YORK • LONDON

Copyright © 1965 by **W.B. Saunders Company**

University Press of America,™ Inc.

4720 Boston Way
Lanham, MD 20706

3 Henrietta Street
London WC2E 8LU England

Library of Congress Cataloging in Publication Data

Gilberstadt, Harold.
    A handbook for clinical and actuarial MMPI
interpretation.

    Bibliography: p.
    Reprint. Originally published: Philadelphia : Saunders,
1965.
    1. Minnesota multiphasic personality inventory. I.
Duker, Jan. II. Title. [DNLM: 1. MMPI. WM 145 G463h
1965a]
BF698.8.M5G5 1965   155.2'83   81–40902
ISBN 0–8191–2257–2 (pbk.)   AACR2

Reprinted by arrangement with

CBS College Publishing

A Handbook for Clinical

and Actuarial MMPI Interpretation

Editor's Foreword

"If all the thousands of clinical hours currently being expended in concocting clever and flowerly personality sketches from test data could be devoted instead to scientific investigation . . . it would probably mean a marked improvement in our net social contribution."*

Thus, in his 1955 presidential address to the Midwestern Psychological Association did Meehl conclude his closely reasoned proposals for the development of cookbooks for certain diagnostic, descriptive, or predictive purposes in clinical work.

Dr. Gilberstadt and Dr. Duker, in the present volume, have produced an excellent example of the kind of handbook Meehl specified. By a combination of clinical and actuarial methods, by use of an extensive sample of hospital records, by careful cross validation techniques, by detailed specification of rules for classification, they have generated a set of major diagnostic and descriptive types. It is important to realize what form of type theory is involved here: "empirically observed collections or sets of traits which recur and serve to sort individuals meaningfully into diagnostic classes" (page 6).

Several features of this monograph are notable. First, it establishes an eminently practical, reliable, and efficient means of providing diagnostic services under conditions of high patient intake and load. Second, it clearly describes a method that can be used or replicated in other clinical settings—a method that truly makes "public the steps of inference employed . . . in arriving at a personality description or a diagnosis" (page 4). Third, it relates the diagnostic categories to symptomatic behavior and terms in common usage, and to alternative psychiatric nomenclature. Fourth, it discusses each type in terms of the relevant research literature in psychology and psychiatry. Finally, the case histories in Appendix II, chosen from a wealth of clinical material, give an immediate sense of reality and dimensionality to the type analyses.

*Meehl, P. E.: Wanted—a good cookbook. American Psychologist, 11:263-272, 1956.

The volume, then, is of greater substance than might be evident by entitling it merely a Handbook. It should be of interest not only to medical and psychological practitioners, but also to those concerned with personality theory, psychometric theory, and abnormal psychology, since these areas derive some of their viability from real clinical data.

University of Minnesota   JOHN G. DARLEY

Preface

The handbook to follow is intended to provide in clear-cut, easily applied form a standard for interpreting and reporting Minnesota Multiphasic Personality Inventory (MMPI) profiles obtained from psychiatric patients for screening and diagnostic purposes. It is designed for use by clinicians in hospitals, clinics, or offices for diagnostic personality screening of incoming patients. It is intended to apply mainly to "admission profiles"; that is, profiles from patients with a test-taking set to seek help either because they are applying for treatment or because they have been newly accepted for treatment. The handbook is also intended as a source book for use in didactic training and as a reference source for research.

Part I presents the rationale of the "cookbook" approach, the method employed to derive the cookbook types, and a description of the cookbook format. Part II presents detailed instructions for interpretation of MMPI profiles by the cookbook method and the cookbook details for 19 particular MMPI profile types which appear to have significance as signs of clinically important syndromes. For each profile type in Part II, the following data will be given: (a) a list of complaints, traits, and symptoms associated with the profile type; (b) a capsule description of the profile type which contains the cardinal features that appear to be most important from a clinical standpoint; and (c) the best psychiatric diagnosis inferred from the present research and alternative diagnoses which reflect actual diagnostic opinions of psychiatric staff.

Following the abbreviated cookbook material for each profile type, a discussion is presented which ties the empirically derived cookbook material to the most relevant writings from the psychological and psychiatric literature. Included in the discussion for each profile type are carefully synthesized clinical descriptive data regarding background, vocational and marital adjustment, and clinical appearance derived from the actual cases of the study. (A brief summary of a typical case for each profile type is included in the Appendix.) Also included in the discussion are hypotheses and generalizations about etiology and dynamics which have implications for personality theory and, particularly, for further research. It should be

vii

emphasized that the 19 profiles were not selected for the handbook necessarily because they were statistically the most frequent (although a sufficiently great frequency was required to provide an adequate sample for
developing the type construct), but because of their value in demonstrating
the relevance of clinically important variables or variables that had particularly high relevance for the MMPI.

Part III includes a summary and conclusions.

The material to follow has been derived from a clinical-statistical
approach to a large pool of psychiatric cases and can easily be applied, in a
manner which will become apparent to the reader, for "actuarial" or "cookbook" personality diagnosis and description based on computer or other
quasimechanical techniques.

Contents

PART THREE: SUMMARY AND CONCLUSIONS

Chapter 5

APPENDIX

PART ONE

Introduction and Method

Chapter 1

Introduction

OVERVIEW

There is great need and demand, particularly in those clinical settings where treatment and disposition plans must be formulated for large numbers of acute or previously undiagnosed psychiatric patients, to have diagnostic instruments with a high degree of utility. Personality tests such as the Minnesota Multiphasic Personality Inventory (MMPI) are relied on heavily even though it has been generally agreed that, despite extensive research efforts, validation is still not complete and entirely satisfactory. Along with the requirement for more adequate validation of personality tests such as the MMPI, a need has been recognized for improved methods of applying the results of personality tests. An important focus on this problem has been provided by the discussions of clinical versus actuarial prediction (Meehl, 1954) and by the appearance of cookbook approaches to personality description based on the MMPI (Symposium, 1962; Marks and Seeman, 1963). In addition, it seems apparent that, with accumulation of validity data and with advances in methodology relative to clinical tests such as the MMPI, some contributions to personality theory which are test-derived should be forthcoming. The present study represents an effort (a) to add to the validity data on the MMPI; (b) to provide the basis for an application of cookbook techniques; and (c) to add some bits of inductively derived knowledge to the body of personality theory.

In his call for MMPI cookbooks, Meehl (1956) presented arguments to show that for given psychometric patterns, personality descriptions should be generated by automatic, mechanical, clerical, "cookbook" procedures. Meehl recommended that such personality cookbooks be constructed of trait descriptions based on average Q-sort placements or on correlational data derived from groups having specified psychometric patterns. This approach has been embodied in the work of Marks and Seeman (1963).

In a recent paper, Hathaway (1962) has argued for a return to a type

3

view of personality in which individuals are grouped into test-determined classes. These classes are then characterized by salient descriptive adjectives suitable to the context in which they are to be applied. Hathaway would require that the test data (input information) on the basis of which classes are formed be objective and suitable to analysis. He would require that the personality descriptions (output information) also be objective. In the intervening step between input data and output data, however, he advocates a clinical approach which permits "the free operation of the psychologist's experience, intuition and judgment." He states: "The chain would be from objective test data input through clinical subjective integration to objective and specific output." The present cookbook has been developed in precisely this fashion.

MMPI profiles (objective test data) constituted the input data on the basis of which individuals were grouped into classes; output consists of descriptive data characterizing the classes. The central step was essentially a clinical one. The evolution of the present cookbook was as follows: As a result of clinical experience, many frequently occurring MMPI profile patterns became very familiar to clinicians. Many of these patterns not only occurred frequently but they also seemed to have particular clinical significance. With experience, the observers noted, and stored away for future use, consistencies in symptom pictures, background histories, behavioral styles, and outcome trends accompanying these profiles. The observers also noted ties to type-constructs inherent in current psychiatric thinking. As experience accumulated, the profile patterns came to serve as signs of syndromes so that given profiles became interpretable not only by established correlations and logical inferences from their scale elevations, but also as signs of personality constructs having broad networks of relationships.

Clinical psychology has been described as an applied science which is part art and part science. In the realm of diagnosis, what this statement may boil down to is that the clinician has not bothered, or has not been able, to make public the steps of inference employed by him in arriving at a personality description or a diagnosis. The problem is not unique to psychologists. Speaking of psychiatric diagnosis, Cobb (1950, p. 104) has stated that "intuition . . . is nothing more than making use of a great experience by short-cut methods that are not conscious."

Many clinicians lack the training and habits of thought to be able to specify the analytical, computer-like cerebral activity interposed between test input and descriptive output. It seems likely that essentially what is involved is access to an apperceptive mass of stored information and a process of successive contrasts between the input data and the stored information. Sometimes it is argued that the clinician, being human, uses himself in the intermediary analytical process which, *ipso facto*, must remain a private and artistic process. This would seem to be an acceptable argument for maintaining the status quo only if it could be shown that the complex analytical activities of the clinician are not ultimately specifiable. If it can be demonstrated at a clinical level that, in principle, the intermediary clinical steps of inference are knowable, there would seem to be little likelihood that any individual clinician, on any basis, would prove superior to the accumulated knowledge that could be placed into a storage system and retrieved systematically.

On occasion, what is labeled as artistic skill may be a kind of legerdemain. A particular expert with a given psychometric device, for example, may learn to recognize signs which have such high probability of being associated with particular syndromes as to be almost pathognomonic. By using the signs, he produces exceptional personality descriptions and predictions, not necessarily from his detailed analysis of the test protocol, or from using himself in an empathic way, but simply from applying a privately held, highly sophisticated construction of the syndrome in response to the sign. Human nature being as it is, it seems likely that many remarkable clinical performances have occurred in this way, with or without realization on the part of the clinician, but with conscious or unconscious reluctance to recognize the source of his powers.

Output in the present cookbook consists not only of specific, objective data such as high frequency traits, modal diagnoses, etc., associated with particular profile types but includes, in addition, general information about the profile types and related syndrome constructs which can serve as a standard by which clinicians can prepare output particularly suited to their own purposes.

INPUT DATA

The MMPI was chosen as the source of input data because: (a) The MMPI is widely used in psychiatric settings, including the setting in which the authors have obtained extensive clinical experience. In this setting alone, over 700 admissions are studied each year. This provides a file of thousands of cases. (b) The MMPI provides totally objective scoring and general suitability as a controlled method of observation. (c) A substantial amount of research relevant to the cookbook approach with the MMPI has already accumulated.

The 550 personality items in the MMPI were empirically culled by Hathaway and McKinley (1951) from prior personality inventories and the existing body of psychiatric knowledge. The items appear to cover the domain of psychiatrically relevant personality traits and symptoms as evenly and thoroughly as was possible at the stage of personality theory in the recent era.

In taking the MMPI, the subject sorts the items into true and false categories. The items sample 26 subject matter categories from the following areas: general health; neurological disturbances, cranial nerve symptoms; sensory, motor, and autonomic nervous system disturbances; physiological disturbances; habit patterns; family and marital problems; occupational and educational questions; sexual, religious, political, and social attitudes; manic and depressive affective responses; obsessive and compulsive symptoms; schizophrenic thinking disturbances; and masculine and feminine interest patterns.

The items are routinely scored to yield a profile consisting of four validity scales and nine clinical scales based originally on the background of Kraepelinian terminology. The validity scales L, F, and K provide measures of test-taking attitude but also yield trait inferences in themselves. When possible, the clinical scales were developed empirically rather than through older armchair methods. For example, when the Hypochondriasis Scale (Hs, Scale 1) was constructed, the test items were administered to a group of hospitalized psychiatric patients who were diagnosed by psychiatric staff as hypochondriacs and to large groups of normals of various categories. Those items which were responded to in a given direction with reliably greater frequency by the hypochondriacs were then counted for the Hypochondriasis Scale. Most normal persons who take the test answer some of these empirically determined "hypochondriacal" items in the scored direction. To exceed the arbitrary limit for normality of two standard deviations above the mean (a score higher than that obtained by 98 percent of the normal samples), however, the male subject must respond to 20 items (less the K-correction) of the Hs scale in the scorable direction. Similarly, the Hysteria Scale (Hy, Scale 3) was constructed by comparing the responses of patients diagnosed as conversion hysteria with the normal samples. With a few exceptions, a similar empirical procedure was employed to develop other clinical scales (Welsh and Dahlstrom, 1956).

In oversimplified terms, the single scale elevations beyond normal limits can be interpreted as follows: L—rigidity or naïveté; F—confused thinking or self-depreciation; K—defensiveness; Hypochondriasis (Hs, Scale 1)—hypochondriasis and body narcissism; Depression (D, Scale 2)—depression; Hysteria (Hy, Scale 3)—repression and denial; Psychopathic Deviate (Pd, Scale 4)—immaturity and impulsiveness; Masculinity-Femininity (Mf, Scale 5)—passivity (for males), interests characteristic of opposite sex; Paranoia (Pa, Scale 6)—sensitivity, hostility; Psychasthenia (Pt, Scale 7)—anxiety, obsessive thinking; Schizophrenia (Sc, Scale 8)—confused, schizoid, bizarre thinking; Mania (Ma., Scale 9)—euphoria, hyperactivity; Social Introversion-Extroversion (Sie, Scale 0)—withdrawal, introversion. Low scales can also be interpreted. For example, low Sie scores are associated with outgoingness and sociableness and low K with "plus-getting," excessive help-seeking.

In the clinical application of MMPI profiles, interpretation usually does not rest upon the elevation of a single score but attention is given to the configuration of all of the scales in the profiles. There are two leading systems for characterizing profiles by codes. In the present instance, a simplified version of Hathaway's profile coding system is used in which profiles are labeled in the order of their scale elevations from highest to lowest beyond the normal limits of T-score 70. For example, if D, Pt, Sc (Scales 2, 7, and 8) were elevated beyond T-score 70 in the order given, the profile would be called a 2-7-8.

INTERMEDIATE TYPE THEORY

The concept of type (or class pattern) is interposed between the input and output data. In the present context, types are conceived of as empirically observed collections or sets of traits which recur and serve to sort individuals meaningfully into diagnostic classes. Loevinger (1957) contrasts class patterns of traits which are present or absent that describe a class of people (e.g., neurotics) with universal traits that are present to a greater or lesser degree in everyone and can be the object of quantitative measurement. The present study deals with the first, the class patterns of traits. No effort has been made to provide quantitative measurements of universal traits.

Traits, from the standpoint of this book, are considered to be summary descriptive terms for behavioral dispositions which may be of diverse kinds but which are meaningfully related one to the other. The trait names have become part of either the general or the technical language because their utility has been inferred from collective experience and their meaning has been validated consensually.

Writers such as Cattell (1946) have made a useful distinction between two kinds of traits: source traits, which are more general and at a deeper level of personality, and surface traits, which are more specific and at a more superficial level. Passivity as a source trait member of a class pattern or type cluster, for example, could generate a number of surface traits such as somatic reactions to stress, interpersonal submissiveness, etc.

The assumption is made that responses to test items are signs of dispositions to behave in certain ways in nontest situations or, in other words, are signs that the individual possesses certain traits. There is the further assumption that a highly consistent tendency to respond to a variety of test items (or signs) empirically associated with a given trait (so that the individual obtains a high score on the test scale constructed to measure the trait) indicates a highly consistent disposition to behave in ways predicted by the trait in nontest situations. In other words, an individual obtaining a high score on a given scale would be predicted to be an extreme deviate with respect to the traits empirically associated with that scale. The demonstration of the validity of these assumptions is, in essence, a major focus of the present work.

A relevant discussion of type theory was presented by Young (1947) who observed that, "confronted with a welter of concrete experiences with specific individuals in a variety of situations—some similar and some dissimilar—men everywhere apparently begin to form general or class ideas about people and their behavior." Among other methods for discovering personality classes, Young described a method advocated many years ago by Zubin (1938) which combines clinical empiricism and statistical method. In this approach, the clinical and common-sense observations of certain recurrent general trait clusters make it possible to classify these repeated features into rough groupings which serve as a first step in the development of types. In the present book, the rough groupings were made by noting consistencies between profile types and trait clusters.

Allport (1961) observed that traits reside in a person but that types reside in some outside point of view. He notes that many types are abstractions created by taking limited aspects of people and forcing them into categories fashioned by the interests and biases of the investigators. Allport is of the opinion that there is a valid approach in which types can be based empirically on the same kind of evidence as are traits. He says that "if by empirical investigation it can be shown that many habits, traits and attitudes are manifestations of a more embracing organization (and if many people are found to have this embracing organization) then these people constitute a type." Allport presents theoretical arguments to illustrate pitfalls even in this approach, however, and concludes that, to preserve the doctrine of empirical type, it is necessary to say that most people are of "mixed" types. In reply to Allport's views, it might be argued that the more extreme personality deviations represented in psychiatric syndromes permit the identification of significant, powerful trait variables which are highly relevant as a basis for typing or for combining into meaningful mixed types but which would not be apparent in groups of more normal, "balanced" individuals.

The present approach does not rest on a predetermined bias regarding the existence of certain personality types but reflects a clinical-statistical investigation of the empirically derived hypothesis that certain frequently recurring MMPI profile patterns are associated with certain trait clusters that are significant and specifiable.

Although it is generally conceded that psychiatric typologies are not completely satisfactory and are poorly validated, it would seem unwarranted to presume that existing psychiatric syndrome constructs, most of which were based on clinical observations of patterns of traits that existed among patients in some real sense, are worthless. Limited samples, theoretical biases, poor communication skill, and poor theory have all resulted in many inadequate typologies, but it would seem to be a mistake to fail to make use of the body of accumulated knowledge about psychiatric syndromes because it is less than perfect.

OUTPUT DATA

The problem of reporting adequately clinical-statistical cookbook information would not seem to differ in essence from the problem of reporting adequately psychological clinical data derived by any other means. Such basic considerations as the purpose of the report and the clarity of communication with potential readers, to name only two considerations, would still be of primary importance.

In the sections to follow, five main categories of cookbook data are included: *first*, the contingency rules that specify the profile of the given type; *second*, the most probable psychiatric diagnosis; *third*, the list of complaints, traits and symptoms associated with the profile of the given type; *fourth*, the cardinal features of the profile type in a capsule description; and *fifth*, interspersed and compared with references to the literature, clinical descriptive excerpts which are synthesized from (a) the background and early history, (b) the educational and vocational adjustment, (c) the heterosexual development and marital adjustment, and (d) the clinical appearance and trait makeup of all of the cases which were in the criterion group of a given type.

Given an MMPI profile which meets the contingency rules for any one of the 19 profile types included in the present cookbook, a clerk or a computer could provide any one or all of the several types of information that have been included. For example, the output could be just the list of statistically frequent traits. This would entail a fairly safe kind of prediction. For each profile type, the list contains several traits with better than chance probability of occurrence. Most of these traits will meaningfully and usefully characterize any profile that fits the rules for the type. Even those traits that are not focal to the case in question will still be highly relevant. (All of the traits that have a high frequency of occurrence for a given profile type are listed, but those traits in the list that have a higher frequency of occurrence for the given profile type than for patients-in-general (Rosen, 1952) should be particularly valuable for differential diagnosis.) The trait list could provide a relatively unambiguous description that could be comprehended clearly by any qualified potential reader of the report. The great weakness of such a report obviously would be its lack of scope. Such a report would not satisfy many potential readers.

An alternative or supplementary approach is to use a profile, after adequate empirical validation, in an actuarial way as a sign of a syndrome. At the present stage of clinical psychology and psychiatry, which many would still characterize as a preclassificatory stage, validation rests on comparatively crude clinical matching procedures. Used as a sign of a diagnostic construct, a profile can yield output ranging from a shorthand diagnostic label to any degree of detail about a syndrome which would seem to be appropriate for a given report. Using profiles in this manner entails certain dangers. Unless actuarial prediction is perfect, which does not seem likely at this stage when only a fraction of possible contingencies have been identified, embarrassing misses could occur. Even if the probability of misses is statistically low, a clinician would tend to be nervous about the possibility of any false positives with the implications of this approach. Thus, if a profile is to be used to generate a diagnostic label, a capsule summary, or an extended clinical description, for maximum safety a psychologist should be interposed between the actuarial input and output processes to screen cases in order to eliminate misses.

To clarify communication about profile types, handbook material has been added to the cookbook sections. In this handbook material, the following information is included for matching and comparison: (1) the diagnostic label and description from the *Diagnostic and Statistical Manual, Mental Disorders,* of the American Psychiatric Association (1952) which best fits each profile type; (2) the synthesized, generalized descriptive excerpts from the criterion cases of the profile type; (3) selected descriptions from the literature which have been judged to be most salient; and (4) relevant MMPI research data. For a psychologist and a reader to communicate clearly, especially if shorthand language such as diagnostic labels is to be used, both would have to be familiar with the profile type construct as elaborated in the handbook.

Since experience has indicated that clinicians tend not to make adequate use of existing diagnostic manuals, it would seem realistic and practical to recommend that, when a clinician obtains a profile that fits the contingency rules for a given profile type, he refer to the handbook in order to select from the potential output those data that best suit the purposes of his report. Of course, he would not be constrained from appending his own ideas, knowledge, or intuition to this process, although he would want to exercise care not to detract from the standard interpretation provided in the cookbook. Obviously, if the psychologist were in a setting where all of his reports were prepared for a single purpose or prepared with a restricted, highly similar set of readers in mind, then given a profile which satisfies the contingencies to serve as a sign of a particular syndrome, the clinician would need only to screen the case for applicability before issuing an already written standard report to his reader.

Interpretation and reporting become more difficult and less comprehensive, however, when the profile to be interpreted does not precisely fit the contingency rules for one of the 19 profile types. With experience in using the cookbook, some clinicians will develop skill in detecting profiles that are near-misses but still lend themselves to application of the cookbook as it has been described. To make the cookbook approach more generally applicable and useful for profiles that do not fit the rules, a set of detailed instructions bearing various codes for interpretation of profiles has been devised and is included in the cookbook.

It should be strongly emphasized that the present cookbook data have been derived from cases seeking admission or recently admitted to a general hospital psychiatry service. This condition provides control for the extremely important variable of test-taking set. Even from this same set of patients, however, MMPI profiles obtained later during treatment, or upon discharge, differ greatly from the admission profiles. It should be further emphasized that such later profiles frequently will not fit the contingencies specifying admission tests. Similarly, tests obtained from individuals of different sex, socioeconomic status, age, etc., might not be included in the specifications for the profile types of the present cookbook. It seems apparent that, within the limits of error inherent in the present procedure, any profile that does fit the contingency rules should be interpretable as specified by the cookbook. Not every individual classifiable into a given category (e.g., pseudoneurotic schizophrenia) will obtain the modal profile for that type so that more than one profile type may signal a given syndrome. If an individual does obtain a profile of given characteristics, then, it is proposed that in the great majority of cases, the cookbook interpretation should be valid and applicable within practical limits regardless of the population characteristics.

Chapter 2

Method of Cookbook Construction and Description of Cookbook Contents

INSTRUCTION SECTION

Preceding the presentation of the 19 profile types in the cookbook will be found the general instructions for application of the cookbook as well as an extensive set of rules for the interpretation of profiles that do not fit the rules for any of the 19 profile types. These rules will yield profile interpretations that are less comprehensive than those for profiles that are exact fits to the profile types, but will permit important diagnostic and descriptive statements to be made about a majority of MMPI profiles obtained from patients being screened for psychiatric treatment. Some of the rules have been inferred from the characteristics of the 19 profile types and others from clinical experience. All of the rules have been tested and cross-validated to some extent on the complete sample of patients admitted to the Minneapolis VA Hospital Psychiatry Service during 1960, but at this stage should be considered incompletely validated.

SELECTION OF PROFILE TYPES

The procedure in selecting the criterion cases on which the cookbook was developed was such that the actuarial data stem from a multiple case history method which is related to a "classical case" approach. Rather than one classical case, however, at least nine or ten cases for each profile type have been used. Each case is highly characteristic of the profile type and has been selected from a much larger pool of possible cases of the profile type by a process of successive refinement (Gilberstadt and Duker, 1960).

The 19 MMPI profiles for which personality descriptions are presented in this cookbook were drawn from a set of specimen profiles that had been accumulated gradually by the authors during their clinical experience on the Psychiatry Service of the Minneapolis VA Hospital. This service is a 100-bed section of a large general hospital. It admits about 60 acute psychiatric cases per month for an average stay of less than two months. The MMPI profiles included in the cookbook had come to attention because of their apparent power as cardinal types in representing trait clusters. High frequency of occurrence was not necessarily a criterion for selection and some profile types originally selected could not be validated because of the paucity of suitable cases.

RULES DEFINING PROFILE TYPES

As will be observed by noting the specificity of the rules that identify each of the profile types in the cookbook which follows, the profiles have been very narrowly defined. Most of the profile-type research with the MMPI has focused on only the most highly elevated one or two scales. In much MMPI research, therefore, profiles carrying such divergent personality descriptions as the 2-7, 2-7-4, and 2-7-8 types presented in this cookbook have been lumped together.

Because of the large number of variables interacting on the MMPI profile, including scale elevation, the problems of profile analysis are complex. Several methods have been suggested for meeting the problems, but the method chosen by the present authors was similar to that proposed by Meehl and Dahlstrom (1960). In this method, rules are derived empirically that will specify the elevation and the interrelationships of the MMPI scales of a particular type of profile and that will exclude profiles assumed not to be of the particular type. The method permits utilization of accumulated clinical experience. The set of specimen profiles was accumulated out of this experience. With these specimen profiles as a starting point, contingency rules were formulated that narrowly specified the characteristics of the profile type. The procedure was as follows:

1. Records were selected from the files for all patients admitted to the Psychiatric Service of the Minneapolis Veterans Administration Hospital and examined by the Psychology Section during the years 1952 to 1957. All patients were male veterans. Cases which met the following criteria were studied:

    a. MMPI administered not more than 21 days before or 21 days after admission.
    b. Age range 20 to 60 years.
    c. Primary diagnosis not brain damage.
    d. MMPI scale T-scores: L=60 or less, F=85 or less, K=70 or less.
    e. Shipley Institute of Living Scale IQ estimate 105 or more.

2. The case records for each of the types were studied in the following manner: First, all cases for the year 1956 whose MMPI profile fit the criteria outlined above were selected. These records were read by the authors. The records consisted of psychiatric discharge summaries and social case history data. The first reading gave a subjective clinical impression

of the patients in the group. The records were then reread and rated on a five-point scale from poor to excellent for goodness of fit to the preliminary subjective clinical formulation. Rules were then revised to eliminate cases that did not seem to fit exceptionally well to the evolving "classic case" picture. Next, all records from the additional years of 1952 and 1953 were read and rules were again refined to eliminate cases that seemed inappropriate. Finally, the records for the remaining three years (1954, 1955, and 1957) were read and cases that did not receive high ratings for the developing types were considered to be misses.

After the profile types had been identified and refined in this way, the admission profiles of patients admitted from 1957 to 1960 who met the five criteria listed above were checked for exact fit to these narrowly specified rules, and rules were refined still further. The profile descriptions presented in this cookbook, including check-list data as well as specimen case histories, were therefore drawn from admissions during the years from 1952 to 1960.

The final set of rules which specify each profile type, along with the mean MMPI profile based on the actual cases of the type, will be found in the beginning of the section of the cookbook devoted to each profile type.

CHECK LIST OF COMPLAINTS, TRAITS, AND SYMPTOMS

The case histories of patients whose admission MMPI profiles fit the rules for the 19 types were read by three judges working independently. For each patient, each judge completed a check list (see Appendix I). This check list was derived from one that had been developed empirically by Cantor (1952), who tallied descriptive terms that had appeared in the discharge summaries of psychiatric patients who had been hospitalized in the Minneapolis VA Hospital. Only those items are included as having characterized a given patient for which two of the three judges checked their occurrence.

The case history folder that the judges used in completing the check list for each patient contained a psychiatric discharge summary and a report of social work interviews with the patient and his relatives. To prevent the judges from being contaminated too heavily with data from the MMPI, they were instructed not to use either references to the psychological report or the report itself as sources of information for the check list.

Judges were instructed to complete the check list only on the basis of the language actually used in case histories and were instructed not to go beyond these data to make inferences. The term "depression," for example, was to be checked only if it had been specifically applied to the patient in the case folder. It was not to be inferred from other descriptive data such as "crying," "slowed," and similar symptoms ordinarily assumed to be indicative of depression.

After a frequency count was completed of check-list items on which at least two of the three judges had agreed for each patient in each of the 19 profile types, the item frequency for the profile type was compared with the item frequency for a representative sample of patients from the Psychiatry Service of the Minneapolis VA Hospital. This "general abnormal" sample had been selected by Rosen (1952), who obtained a random sample of 250 cases representative of all patients admitted during a two-year period ending in October, 1951, who had obtained valid MMPI profiles (among other tests) within 15 days of admission and who were not in a postelectro-shock state. Every fifth case of Rosen's sample, arranged alphabetically, was chosen for the present representative sample. This procedure yielded a sample of 100 cases which did not deviate significantly from the original representative sample of 250 cases (Gilberstadt, 1952). The check list was applied to the 100 cases by three judges in the same manner as has been described above and the frequency for each item was recorded. (See Appendix I.) The frequency of each check-list item for each of the 19 profile types was compared with the frequency of each item for the general abnormal sample for significance of differences by a nomograph (Lawshech and Baker, 1950). The complaints, traits, and symptoms listed in the cookbook for each profile type are the check-list items which showed a statistically reliable difference (.05 level) between the item frequency for a given profile type and the item frequency for the general abnormal sample. These are the items which are most valuable for differential diagnosis.

In addition to these check-list items which differentiate the patients of a given profile type from patients in general, there are items that occur in the records of patients of a given profile type with high frequency but that are also high frequency or "high base-rate" items for patients in general. Since these items are of value for description, although not for differential diagnosis, they also are included in the cookbook lists of complaints, traits, and symptoms if they occurred in 50 per cent or more of the patients. These high base-rate items have been enclosed in parentheses to distinguish them from the items which were more frequent for the patients in the profile type than for patients in general.

DIAGNOSIS

The sections in the cookbook that provide recommendations for psychiatric diagnosis contain two categories of information. Under the heading "diagnosis" for each profile type will be found the authors' recommendation for diagnosis based on intensive *post hoc* study of the cases in the profile type. Under the heading "alternative diagnosis" will be found the most frequent discharge summary diagnoses (other than the diagnosis being proposed from the present study) actually given to the patients at discharge by the psychiatric staff. In most instances, the contrast is due to a difference in emphasis on particular state or symptom variables which were observed in various patients of a given type by the physician making the diagnosis. It is proposed that the authors' diagnoses will increase the reliability of diagnosis and will bear a closer relationship to diagnostic constructs from the literature because they eliminate individual biases and add the uniformity of actuarial prediction.

CARDINAL FEATURES

The section of the cookbook for each profile type labeled "cardinal features" is the product of an effort, largely clinical in nature, to extract from the more extensive history and clinical data characterizing each profile type the most salient facts and the data that most quickly communicate the essence of the patients' personality and adjustment problems.

DISCUSSION SECTIONS

The discussion that follows the cookbook summary data for each type is intended to elaborate the constructs implied in the summary data, to give the details that formed the basis of the summaries, and last, but not least, to provide a source of material about the profile type on which clinicians can draw for clinical, didactic, or research purposes. References included in the discussion section were chosen for two major reasons: (1) they appeared to be classical writings that have had considerable influence; and (2) there was a close correspondence between the observations in the literature cited and the empirical findings in the present work.

PART TWO

Cookbook

Chapter 3

Instructions for Application
of Cookbook

NOTE: This cookbook is based on the assumption that the MMPI profile has been obtained from a patient or client presenting himself for help to a hospital, clinic, or practicing clinician.

PREPARATION OF MMPI PROFILE

1. Score profile according to standard directions (Hathaway and McKinley, 1951).

2. Draw profile on profile sheet.

T-scores can be read from margins of profile. T-scores are included on the profile sheet because they indicate how much the score obtained on any scale deviates from the scores obtained by the control samples of nonhospitalized normal individuals on whom the test was standardized. The derivation of the T-scores is based on the characteristics of the normal curve. A T-score of 50 is equivalent to the score greater than that obtained by 50 percent of the normal sample. A T-score of 60 is equivalent to that score which is greater than the score obtained by 84 percent of the normal sample. A T-score of 70 is equivalent to the score that is greater than the score obtained by 98 percent of the normal sample. A T-score of 70 is arbitrarily defined as the upper limit of normality for each of the MMPI scales. This limit is indicated on the profile sheet by the upper heavy black line extending across the profile. (The middle heavy black line is drawn at T-score 50. The lower heavy black line is drawn at T-score 30. T-score 30 deviates from average in the low direction to the same degree that T-score 70 deviates in the high direction.) The scores that exceed T-score 70 are particularly important for cookbook interpretation because they form the basis for the coding of the profiles.

3. Code profile.

Along the top of the profile sheet, the clinical scales (beginning with Hs + .4K) are lettered by abbreviations of the scale names (such as Hs for Hypochondriasis and D for Depression) but also are numbered so that Hy is Scale 3 and Pd is Scale 4, etc. The numbers rather than the letters are used for coding. To arrive at the code for entering the present cookbook, list, in descending order of elevation, the numbers of the clinical scales on the profile sheet that are elevated over T-score 70. For example, if D is at T-score 89, Pt is at T-score 79, and Hy is at T-score 71, these being the only clinical scales over T-score 70, the profile will be coded as a 2-7-3. This kind of notation has been used for the labeling of the 19 profile types in the section to follow.

4. Inspect validity scales.

The four scales on the profile to the left of the vertical line are the validity scales. If L or K is over T-score 70, the description "extreme defensiveness" may be reported but no cookbook interpretation can be given (unless profile is of 8-1-2-3 code type). It should be noted that a profile might still be used in a noncookbook approach, but only by a skilled clinical synthesis with other test or history data about the patient.

5. Refer to age and IQ.

If the patient is older than 60 or if his verbal IQ is less than 105 on tests such as the WAIS (or IQ estimates calibrated to the WAIS), the clinician should use caution in applying the cookbook. Even with profiles which fit all of the rules for one of the 19 profile types, the more age exceeds 60 and IQ is under 105, the less accurate the cookbook description is likely to be.

INTERPRETATION OF MMPI PROFILE

1. Interpret profile by code.

Profiles for the 19 MMPI profile types in the following section are ordered according to the first digit of their codes. Where there is more than one profile type with the same first digit in the code, profiles are ordered by the first plus succeeding digits of the code: 2-7, 2-7-4, 2-7-8, etc. If the code of a given profile matches the code digits for one of the 19 types included in the following cookbook section, check to see if the rules for the code type are met. If the rules are satisfied, select output from the cookbook details listed under the code-type.

Interpretation based on the order of elevation of scales beyond T-score 70, that is, the code-type, tends to be the most powerful way of interpreting profiles even when profiles do not fit precisely the particular set of rules. (It should be remembered that these rules were devised for selecting "classical" cases of the respective types.) Thus, if a profile is a near-miss because it has one scale too high or too low or because it has an extraneous scale interpolated in the code (the latter event is actually most easily determined by visual inspection of the profile), check potential cookbook description by outside information from history or other testing and apply cookbook details in modified form as indicated by available information.

2. Interpret profile by "state rules."

Many of the profiles that do not meet the exact rules by which the profiles can serve as signs of the syndromes or diagnostic constructs of the 19 types detailed in this cookbook are obtained from patients whose main complaint or adjustment difficulty is a disturbance of emotional state. (States are considered to be emotional disturbances of more or less transient or time-limited nature in contrast to the more enduring behavioral dispositions implied by the use of the term "traits.") From a clinical diagnostic standpoint, these disturbances usually take precedence over other aspects of personality such as "character type," for example, and are important to diagnose since the major reason for hospitalization, or the main focus of treatment, may be the alleviation of the state of emotional disequilibrium. Thus, if profiles do not lend themselves to the more comprehensive kind of interpretation yielded by the procedures under the preparation of the profile, the next step is to try them for fit to the following set of diagnostic rules for state disturbances:

STATE RULES

Depressive State: (T-scores)
1. D 70 to 79, Ma less than 40
2. D 80 to 99, Ma less than 50
3. D 100+, Ma less than 60

Anxiety State: (T-scores)
1. Pt 70 to 79 (moderate)
2. Pt 80 to 89 (marked)
3. Pt 90+ (severe)

Agitated State: (T-scores)
1. Pd and Pa greater than 65

Manic State: (T-scores)
1. Ma greater than 70, D less than 55

If any of the three rules for depression are satisfied, diagnose "depressive reaction." If any of the rules for anxiety are satisfied (in effect, according to the elevation of the Pt scale), diagnose "anxiety reaction" (moderate, marked, or severe, as indicated). Similarly, diagnose agitated or manic states if those rules are satisfied.

3. Interpret profile by combinations of scale elevations.

Profiles that cannot be interpreted by code-type as indicated under the preparation of MMPI profile, whether or not they are interpreted by the "state rules," can be interpreted by combinations of scales elevated over T-score 70. (Possible interpretations of single scale elevations over T-score 70 have already been described [p. 6]. The following list of rules should be tried consecutively. *Start with the rules rather than the profile elevations!* Each time a rule fits the profile, select the statement accompanying the rule for part of the profile interpretation.

RULES FOR PROFILE INTERPRETATION

(Use with extreme caution or not at all if K or L T-score is 70 or more and F is greater than T-score 100. Proceed through list consecutively. Except for rule 16, rules do not hold if patient has organic brain syndrome.)

Scales greater than T-score 70	*Interpretive statement*
1. 1 & 2 (in order; highest elevations)	Look for depression
2. 1, 2, & 3 (in order)	Look for hypochondriasis
3. 1, 2, 3, & 4	Look for oral hostile-dependent alcoholic
4. 1, 2, 3 (in order) & 8	Look for probable somatic delusions
5. 1 & 3 (profile peaks; Ma less than 60)	Look for hysteroid, passive, somatizing individual with conversion reaction
6. 1, 3, 2 (in order; Ma less than 60)	Look for reactive depression in passive personality
7. 1, 6 (if 4 less than 70)	Look for paranoid schizophrenia
8. 2 & 1 (in order; only scales above 70)	Look for paranoid schizophrenia, organic brain syndrome, old age, etc., but do not interpret profile
9. 2, 3 (only scales 70 or above)	Look for depressive reaction with anxiety in hysteroid personality
10. 2, 4 (only scales 70 or above)	Look for reactively depressed, passive-aggressive personality
11. 2, 7 (only scales 70 or above)	Look for anxiety, depression in obsessional type
12. 2, 7 (profile peaks) & 4	Look for chronically depressed, anxious, immature chronic alcoholic
13. 2, 6	Look for agitated depression
14. 2, 7, & 8 (Sie above 65) (If 7 & 8 above 2, rule out psychotic depression)	Look for schizophrenic reaction
15. 2, 8 (profile peaks)	Look for depressive reaction, possibly schizo-affective type
16. 2, 9	Look for organic brain syndrome
17. 2, 0 (profile peaks)	Look for withdrawn, schizoid personality
18. 3, 1	(See 1-3)
19. 3, 1, & 2 (in order)	(See 1-3-2)
20. 3, 2 (in order; only scales 70 or above)	Look for situational maladjustment in hysteroid inadequate character
21. 3, 4	Look for emotionally unstable personality
22. 3, 5 (males)	Look for deep-seated psychosexual passivity
23. 3, 9	Look for hostile, emotionally labile personality
24. 4, 2	(See 2, 4)
25. 4, 3	(See 3, 4)
26. 4, 5	Look for narcissistic character
27. 4, 6 (only scales above 70)	Look for paranoid state

Scales greater than T-score 70	*Interpretive statement*
28. 5, 4	(See 4, 5)
29. 5, 6 (only scales above 65)	Look for paranoid state
30. 6, 4	(See 4, 6)
31. 6, 5	(See 5, 6)
32. 6, 8 (except when 4 is 70 or above)	Look for paranoid schizophrenia
33. 7 (if 7 peak)	Look for phobic symptoms
34. 7, 2	(See 2, 7)
35. 7, 8	Look for schizoid obsessional thinking
36. 7, 9 (profile peaks; if not organic and can disregard 2-9 rule or if not schizophrenic by 6-8 rule)	Look for manic-depressive, manic type
37. 8, 2	(See 2, 8)
38. 8, 4 (profile peaks)	Look for immaturity, alcoholism, sexual deviation, paranoid trends
39. 8, 6	(See 6, 8)
40. 8, 7	(See 7, 8)
41. 8, 9 (profile peaks)	Look for catatonic state

Chapter 4

Cookbook of 19 Profile Types

1-2-3 TYPE

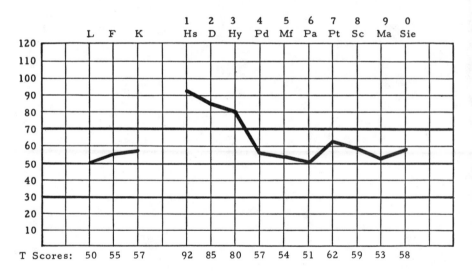

T Scores: 50 55 57   92 85 80 57 54 51 62 59 53 58

Rules

1. Hs, D, and Hy over T-score 70
2. Hs > D > Hy
3. No other scales over T-score 70
4. L—T-score 65 or less, F—T-score 85 or less, K—T-score 70 or less

Mean Profile (N=11)

Diagnosis

Psychophysiological reaction.

Alternative Diagnoses

Anxiety reaction; depressive reaction.

Complaints, Traits, and Symptoms

Abdominal pain	Irritable
Anorexia, nausea, vomiting	Nervousness
Dizziness	Sexual difficulty
Ear complaint	Weak, tired, fatigued
Headache	Worrying
Insomnia	(Anxiety)

Cardinal Features

Somatic symptoms usually of autonomic nervous system origins (as shown above). React to emotion-producing life stresses with physiological symptoms that may appear rather than usual affect (e.g., depression).

Lack aggressiveness. Lack sexual drive. Stable work and marital adjustment.

DISCUSSION

Writings from the field of psychosomatic medicine provide the most valuable source of data for illuminating the 1-2-3 profile type, which represents a psychophysiological reaction.

The official *Diagnostic Manual* of the American Psychiatric Association (1952) describes the category of psychophysiological autonomic and visceral disorders as follows (p. 29):

> These reactions represent the visceral expression of affect which may be thereby largely prevented from being conscious. The symptoms are due to a chronic and exaggerated state of the normal physiological expression of emotion, with the feeling, or subjective part, repressed. Such long continued visceral states may eventually lead to structural changes. . . .
>
> Differentiation is made from conversion reactions by (1) involvement of organs and viscera innervated by the autonomic nervous system, hence not under full voluntary control or perception; (2) failure to alleviate anxiety; (3) physiological rather than symbolic origin of symptoms; (4) frequent production of structural changes which may threaten life.

The high-frequency symptoms of the 1-2-3 type include abdominal pain, anorexia, nausea, vomiting, anxiety, blindness—eye complaint, ear complaint, depression, dizziness, headache, insomnia, irritability, nervousness, sexual difficulty, tension, weak—tired—fatigued, and worrying. This list virtually duplicates that provided by Weiss and English (1957, p. 90) in their discussion of psychosomatic diagnosis.

Case history data for the 1-2-3 type contain evidence of a trend for the patients to be described as physiologically weak and behaviorally maladjusted in childhood. In several instances there was evidence of domination by older brothers. Parental relationships varied. Some parents were stern; some mothers were indulgent while others were rejecting. No predominant pattern of child-parent relationships prevailed.

Later in life, employment in trades predominated, with occupations such as carpentry, truck driving, tailoring, or barbering being modal. The frequent self-employment in one-man businesses perhaps was related to dominance-submission problems in relation to other people. Vocational histories showed considerable stability and, perhaps, excessive reluctance to change occupations.

At the time of hospitalization, the 1-2-3 type patients were described by adjectives such as shy, timid, guilty, depressed, irritable, tense, nervous, worrying, and dependent. Other family members frequently were reported to have similar symptoms and traits. These patients often showed childish fearfulness. Often they fought with their own children at the level of siblings. Because of their lack of assertiveness, they tended to be dominated by wives and relatives. Some wives complained of their husband's lack of aggressiveness, while others reacted with an understanding, nurturant attitude. Inadequate sexual performance and lack of sexual satisfaction were frequently reported for these patients.

The modal patient of this type was described as physically slight and "nondescript looking." There seemed to be a lack of stamina and stress tolerance prior to hospitalization. Common also were fears about health and phobic attitudes about death and chronic illness. In most instances, it was difficult for these patients to accept the possibility that their symptoms had an emotional tie.

The 1-2-3 case history findings, in general, lend support for a hypothesis that there is a genetic predisposition to physiological disturbances of autonomic nervous system origins. The role of learning, however, should not be underemphasized. Weiss and English have stated that it is usually the family group that harbors the emotional tensions out of which the patient's illness has developed. Meehl (1962, p. 64) has discussed the distinction between psychosomatic phenomena and conversion symptoms in the framework of learning theory:

> The former are respondents and are therefore not "purposive." The latter are operant and are "purposive." The question "What is Mr. X getting out of his stomach ulcer" is not only scientifically unsound but partakes of a certain element of injustice. I don't think it is always correct to say that the patient is getting anything out of his ulcer, although of course even an ulcer (like a conversion symptom) may provide secondary gain. But there is no good evidence that conditioned respondents can be strengthened, or their strength maintained, by reward; so that the secondary gains of a psychosomatic symptom are prognostically of less importance because they do not, theoretically, contribute to symptom maintenance.

Extensive discussions of the mechanisms of symptom formation are provided by writers on psychosomatic medicine. Particularly valuable are the accounts of Alexander and French (1948), Cobb (1950), Weiss and English (1957), and Wolff et al. (1950).

It should be noted that psychosomatic disorders are not limited to the profile type above. The sections to follow will include two other profiles of the 1-2-3 pattern, but the descriptions will show the effect of other scale elevations, in one instance of elevation on Scale 4 (Pd) and in the other instance of elevation on Scale 7 (Pt). These types do not exhaust the possibilities. In a study of patients with neurodermatitis, for example, Gilberstadt (1962) found a modal profile characterized by elevations on Scales 1 and 3, but within normal limits, and a subgroup with elevated Scale 4. Sullivan and Welsh (1952) developed a set of five configural signs to identify psychosomatic ulcer cases. These signs included Scale 1 higher than Scales 2, 3, 7, and 8 and Scale 2 higher than Scale 3. The profile for the 1-2-3 type described above meets all five specifications. Dahlstrom and Welsh (1960, p. 353) report a study in which headache patients were found to show the same configuration identified by Sullivan and Welsh.

In their discussions of major configural patterns, Dahlstrom and Welsh (1960, p. 167) summarize a number of studies on patient groups with 1-2 MMPI codes. Several of these studies report findings which reinforce those for the 1-2-3 type. Especially relevant are studies by Guthrie (1949) and Halbower (1955). Guthrie reported on a large subgroup of patients with 1-2 patterns seen by an urban internist. These patients presented numerous complaints, chiefly of abdominal pathology. Halbower asked therapists to provide Q-sort descriptions of VA Mental Hygiene Clinic patients with narrowly specified 1-2-3 MMPI profiles. These patients presented themselves as organically ill and manifested either a somatization reaction or other psychophysiological reaction. These patients presented a general hypochondriacal picture in which complaints of pain, easy fatiguability, and weariness were prominent. The patients were described as hypersensitive and they overevaluated minor dysfunctions. Meehl (1951) also reports that the most prominent feature in these patients is pain. Complaints center around the viscera in contrast to the patients with 1-3 profiles, who report difficulties in the peripheral organs and central nervous system. This same discrepancy in symptom locale can be noted in the present 1-2-3 type and the 1-3-2 type to be reported later.

1-2-3-4 TYPE

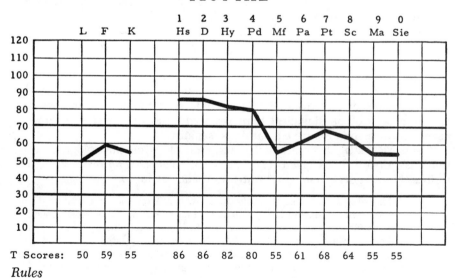

T Scores: 50 59 55   86 86 82 80 55 61 68 64 55 55

Rules

1. Hs, D, Hy, and Pd greater than T-score 70 and higher than all other scales
2. Sie less than T-score 70
3. L, F, and K less than T-score 70 unless two or more scales greater than 100 in which case F less than T-score 80

Mean Profile (N=36)

Diagnoses

Personality trait disturbance with alcoholism, anxiety, depression, and psychophysiological reaction.

Alternative Diagnoses

Anxiety reaction; depressive reaction; psychophysiological reaction with personality trait disturbance.

Complaints, Traits, and Symptoms

Anorexia, nausea, vomiting	Nervousness
Assaultive	Poor financial status
Combative when drunk	Poor work adjustment
Conflict with wife	Suicide attempt
Epigastric complaints	Suspicious
Heavy drinking	Tension
Hostile	Ulcer
Insomnia	Weak, tired, fatigued
Irritable	(Depression)
Mother domineering	

Cardinal Features

Severe alcoholism. Orally fixated. Demanding and dependent to such degree that they are constantly frustrated. Act out with assaultiveness and hostility particularly toward women such as wives or girlfriends. Also develop somatic symptoms, especially ulcers and gastric disturbances, seemingly in reaction to stress or frustration.

DISCUSSION

The presence of the 1-2-3 elevation would suggest a strong psychosomatic element in the 1-2-3-4 type. The elevation of 4 (Pd) would add the element of personality disorder. This profile type therefore combines the elements both of physiological hyperreactivity and of defective character development seen in the psychopathic personality.

The APA *Diagnostic Manual* description of psychophysiological reactions has already been given. (See page 25.) The *Diagnostic Manual* describes the category personality trait disturbance as follows (p. 36):

> This category applies to individuals who are unable to maintain their emotional equilibrium and independence under minor or major stress because of disturbances in emotional development. Some individuals fall into this group because their personality pattern disturbance is related to fixation and exaggeration of certain character and behavior patterns; others, because their behavior is a regressive reaction due to environmental or endopsychic stress.

In addition, the *Diagnostic Manual* states that the clinical picture may show a superimposed anxiety reaction.

The case histories of the 1-2-3-4 type offer support for the hypothesis that there may be a genetic basis for their physiological stomach disturbances. Fathers and siblings were also frequently reported to have epigastric disturbances as well as alcoholism. An oft cited study by Weiner et al. (1957) provides some support for the hypothesis of genetic origins. They obtained serum pepsinogen levels and psychological tests on 2073 draftees to test the hypothesis that the hypersecretor, like the patient with duodenal ulcer, would exhibit evidences of intense infantile oral dependent wishes, marked "immaturity," tendencies to please and placate, and difficulties revolving particularly around the management of oral impulses and hostility. On the basis of these postulated traits by majority opinion of three judges, they correctly identified 71 percent of the hypersecretors. They report that studies on siblings and twins reveal that the secretory capacity of the gastric mucosa as gauged by the serum pepsinogen concentration is genetically determined. They conclude that the secretory capacity of the stomach with which the child is born may play a significant role in his relationship with that environment. These elements would appear to be highly characteristic of the 1-2-3-4 profile type.

In their discussion of the "protective reaction patterns" of offense, Wolff et al. (1950) provide insight into the learning mechanism involved in the conditioning of the stomach and duodenum. Hunger is accompanied by. hypermotility, hyperemia, and hyperactivity of the stomach. The hungry infant who reacts with loud cries to get milk from his mother and is frustrated may be setting the pattern for the man who reacts with excessive motility, engorgement, and hyperactivity of gastric mucosa when longing for something he cannot get.

The nature of the interaction of this somatic predisposition with environmental conditioning can be inferred from the relatively high frequency of dominating mothers and of early childhood deprivation evident in the 1-2-3-4 case histories. In only one of 36 cases was there a suggestion of sound, normal parents. Evidence for too much or too little satisfaction of childhood dependency strivings was present. Oversolicitous mothers were most frequent. Occasionally such oversolicitousness was associated with weakness or frailty in the child. Often reported was stern discipline and a lack of affection from parents. Some mothers "ran around." Many fathers acted-out with drinking and sexual affairs. Some were directly rejecting and others died while the patients were young. Sometimes these patients appeared to have been lost in the shuffle of a large family. Many of these patients were behavior problems as children. The persisting dependency strivings were demonstrated by several patients who continued to live with their parents even after marriage.

The marital relationships of these patients clearly revealed the traits emphasized by Weiner et al. (1957) and by Wolff et al. (1950). Almost all of these patients were severe, chronic alcoholics. They were demanding and oral-dependent to such an extent that wives were unable to satisfy their many demands. Frequently, these patients reacted to the resulting frustrations with extreme hostility. Often they beat their wives, and even in the hospital the 1-2-3-4 patients were frequently noted to be especially demanding. Consistent with profile indications of immaturity and personality defects, these patients often were irresponsible in marital obligations. Often they married divorced women and had conflicts with their stepchildren. Very often they were reported to be jealous and suspicious of their wives. In the unmarried patients there was frequent history of hostility and physical abuse directed at girlfriends. The extreme instance of a poor heterosexual relationship was presented by one patient of this type who shot his pregnant wife.

Oral fixations often seemed to carry over into the vocational sphere. Several of these patients worked in food processing or food serving occupations while two were pharmacists. Most of the patients worked in low-level laboring or semiskilled jobs and showed a marked lack of persistence. This appeared to be a lifelong pattern. About half of these patients were high school dropouts; several had quit in the eleventh grade of high school.

The most frequent symptom at the time of hospitalization was severe alcoholism. About one-half of the patients complained of stomach distress or had a history of ulcers and/or gastrectomies. Other somatic complaints included headaches, backaches, blackouts, and shoulder pains. Symptoms of depression such as insomnia and anorexia were very frequent. History of a suicide attempt or serious suicidal intention was obtained from about 20 percent of the group. Typical abnormal traits were shyness, irritability, worrying, tension, low frustration tolerance, and rage reactions. Impulsiveness and authority problems were frequently mentioned.

The 1-2-3-4 profile type is one of several in the present cookbook in which heavy drinking occurred as a symptom. It will be seen that Scale 4 also appears as a prominent elevation in these other profiles. This observation is consistent with that of other investigators. In reviewing the MMPI findings in addiction, Dahlstrom and Welsh (1960, p. 322) state that the appearance of a strong psychopathic trend is one of the most persistent findings in studies of diagnosed alcoholics. They cite a number of studies which reported findings indicating that Scale 4 elevations reflect one important source of potentiality for developing dependence upon alcohol. In several of these studies, a neurotic component appeared, with Scale 4 occurring as a secondary elevation below the neurotic triad. Dahlstrom and Welsh (1960, p. 323) comment that "this component of Scale 4 tends to distinguish them from neurotics without histories of significant dependence upon alcohol." The present findings with regard to the 1-2-3 elevation, however, would suggest that, rather than characterizing these elevations as "neurotic," a more accurately descriptive characterization would be "psychophysiological hyper-reactivity."

1-2-3-7 TYPE

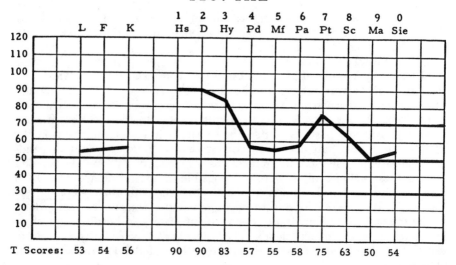

				1	2	3	4	5	6	7	8	9	0
	L	F	K	Hs	D	Hy	Pd	Mf	Pa	Pt	Sc	Ma	Sie

T Scores: 53 54 56   90 90 83 57 55 58 75 63 50 54

Rules

1. Hs, D, Hy, and Pt over T-score 70
2. Hs and D greater than Hy
3. Hs, D, and Hy greater than Pt
4. Ma less than T-score 60
5. Sie less than T-score 70

Mean Profile (N=11)

Diagnosis

Psychophysiological reaction with anxiety in a passive-dependent personality.

Alternative Diagnosis

Psychophysiological reaction.

Complaints, Traits, and Symptoms

Anorexia, nausea, vomiting	Nervousness
Anxiety	Numbness
Back pain	Passive
Dependent	Tension
Epigastric complaints	Worrying
Inadequate	(Depression)

Cardinal Features

Focus on physical complaints. Chronic symptoms of autonomic nervous system origins. Actual chronic organic illness as well as hypochondriacal fixations.

Weak, fearful, highly inadequate. When patients regress, they become unable to take ordinary stresses and simple, everyday responsibilities. May become unable to work and have many years of unproductiveness. May try to perpetuate role of weak, helpless child if wife is strong, adequate, and protective. Moody. Interpersonal relationships inadequate. May become dependent on alcohol or drugs.

DISCUSSION

It will be noted that the 1-2-3-7 patients, although highly similar, differ from the 1-2-3 group in the higher frequency of traits such as anxiety, tension, back pain, chest pain, dependency, and inadequacy. The 1-2-3 component of the profile would suggest a psychophysiological component and the 7 elevation would suggest anxiety and tension. The trait frequency list bears this out. There is also greater predisposition to develop back and chest pain rather than abdominal pain, dizziness, headache, and fatigue and more frequent mention in the case histories of organic illness items such as arthritis, gallbladder disease, gastric surgery, and lung surgery, reflecting a greater incidence of actual organ breakdown.

The APA *Diagnostic Manual* description of psychophysiological reactions has already been given. (See page 25.) The equally relevant passive-dependent type of personality trait disturbance is described as follows (p. 37):

> This reaction is characterized by helplessness, indecisiveness, and a tendency to cling to others as a dependent child to a supporting parent.

The fearfulness of the 1-2-3-7 patients probably reflects attitudes learned early in life. Items such as the death of an older brother by drowning during childhood or a mother who was frightened easily when her children were hurt after one child was killed in a farm accident suggest conditioned learning during childhood as one origin of the fearfulness. As in the 1-2-3 group, the patients frequently came from very large families. There were a large number of parents described as "normal" or "good" among this group although some parents were alcoholic. The lifelong nature of the fearful attitudes was exemplified by one patient who as a child vomited whenever faced with heavy work and another who was afraid to read in school because he feared that he would not do well.

Upon admission to the hospital, a typical description of these patients was "anticipates trouble at every turn and magnifies small problems into overwhelming evidence that he is inadequate." Not only were these patients markedly unable to assert themselves and to take responsibility, but after the onset of illness they frequently regressed to the point where they were unable to work and had many years with little productive employment. At the other extreme were some individuals who seemed to cling to jobs for an unusually long number of years because of inertia and fearfulness about changing.

Most frequently there was marriage to a stronger woman who protected and shielded the patient. Sometimes heterosexual liaisons were of an unusual type such as marrying a younger woman with an illegitimate child or living with a divorcee and her children. In any case, the patients often seemed to be trying to perpetuate the role of weak, helpless children.

Occasionally, these patients satisfied dependency strivings with alcohol or drug addiction. Interpersonal relationships were usually poor. Frequent traits included irritableness, quietness, lack of confidence, indecisiveness, hypochondriasis, worrying, and guilt related to feelings of inadequacy.

Writers on psychophysiological reactions strongly emphasize the interaction between constitution, early conditioning, and life experiences. Kempf (1958, p. 168) states:

> The stresses are carried by the autonomic-motivating system. Cardiac angina, arterial hypertension, asthma, anemia, nephritis, adrenal exhaustion, gastric ulcer, colitis, impotency, sterility, amenorrhea, diabetes, hyperthyroidism, headache, insomnia, apoplexy, are some of the costs. Each person in his characteristic attitude in relation to his work, his family, his boss and competitors, tends to stress some organ more than others. It grows hypertrophic if overworked, hypotrophic if inhibited. A progressive vicious circle is established that tends to complete breakdown and death if not properly treated at the psychophysiological level. Most physicians are educated to think physiologically and surgically in treating diseased organs without consideration of the social attitudes and working situation of the patient.

One of the four MMPI profile types for which Halbower (1955) developed a cookbook description was coded 1-2-3 with Scale 7 above 70. These patients complained of pain, weakness, and easy fatiguability. Therapists described them as lacking in insight and resistant to interpretations that their symptoms were related to emotional difficulties. They were also described as passive, dependent, and repressive.

1-3-2 TYPE

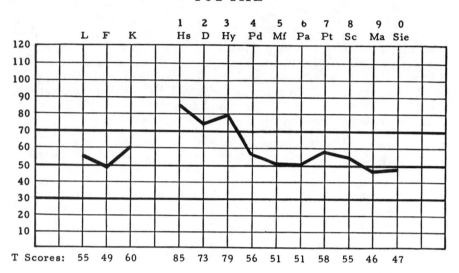

T Scores: 55   49   60   85   73   79   56   51   51   58   55   46   47

Rules

1. Hs, D, and Hy over T-score 70
2. Hs and Hy greater than D
3. No other scales over T-score 70
4. D 5 or more T-scores greater than Pt
5. Ma T-score 60 or below

Mean Profile (N=19)

Diagnosis

   Psychoneurosis, conversion reaction with depression.

Alternative Diagnoses

   Psychophysiological reaction; anxiety reaction.

Complaints, Traits, and Symptoms

Anorexia, nausea, vomiting	Irritable
Back pain	Passive
Chest pain	Tension
Dependent	Weak, tired, fatigued
Headaches	(Anxiety)

Cardinal Features

   Hysteroid, passive-dependent character. Extroverted. Sociable, well-liked until they show irritability and "chuck-it-all" symptoms accompanying reactive depression. Repression and denial result in strong rejection of idea that symptoms have psychological etiology. Under stress, break down with psychosomatic illness or conversion symptoms. Highly conforming and conventional in work and marital adjustment.

DISCUSSION

This profile type represents the "conversion valley" pattern. Since the 1-3 code is one of the most frequent two-point combinations in normal groups as well as in psychiatric groups, it has been rather widely described (Dahlstrom and Welsh, 1960, p. 170). Central in these descriptions, and in the present cookbook description, are repressive defenses, passive modes of behavior, dependency strivings, and denial of emotional difficulties.

In the present study, as in others, the modal diagnosis for these patients was conversion reaction. In the *Diagnostic Manual* of the American Psychiatric Association, this reaction is described as follows (p. 32):

> Instead of being experienced consciously (either diffusely or displaced, as in phobias) the impulse causing the anxiety is "converted" into functional symptoms in organs or parts of the body, usually those that are mainly under voluntary control. The symptoms serve to lessen conscious (felt) anxiety and ordinarily are symbolic of the underlying mental conflict. Such reactions usually meet immediate needs of the patient and are, therefore, associated with more or less obvious "secondary gain."

Examination of the background data for the 1-3-2 type provides some clues as to the possible nature of the childhood learning situation. These data suggest that the syndrome seen in the 1-3-2 profiles results from the effects of repression as a reaction to severe childhood rejection and deprivation. These patients appear to use hysteroid repression and passive solutions to problems, devices probably learned in childhood to cope with environments characterized by emotional and physical deprivation. Frequently described are poor fathers, fathers who were alcoholic or emotionally ill, fathers who died, immoral families, strict, rigid families lacking in affection, and mothers who died.

The 1-3-2 patients tend to be highly passive and conforming. These patients have good work histories unless they "throw in the sponge" because they feel unable to function any longer.

The 1-3-2 patients relate in marriage in a passive and dependent way. There are two frequent patterns. Usually the patients strongly protest that there are no marital problems and that their marriage is perfect or, less frequently, they show an immature, dependent kind of hostility toward wives to the point where wives have threatened to leave (at which time the patients were often shocked into a more positive attitude).

Largely because of a passive-dependent attitude, these patients often reject their children, as they themselves were rejected, and frequently the children react with physical sickness and adjustment difficulties.

The wives, as do wives of other hysteroid patient types, show a high incidence of being capable, attractive, adaptable, well-liked, and sociable. Many hold jobs at which they display considerable competence.

The 1-3-2 patients have many somatic complaints of neuromuscular system origins, with back, stomach, leg, throat, and musculoskeltal symptoms such as arthritis most frequent. They have histories of tendencies to break down with psychomatic illnesses under stress.

The 1-3-2 patients appear to be showing, in the context of hysteroid character structure, reactive depressions. They show the familiar symptoms of reactive depression: being slowed up, passive, irritable, "chuck-it-all" attitudes, disgusted, discouraged, tired, depressed, feeling that life is all over, and feeling sorry for themselves.

In addition to evidences of much repression, these patients show marked attitudes of denial and feel that all their troubles are somatic in origin. They reject the idea of psychological etiology and of psychotherapeutic intervention for the treatment of their symptoms.

They are usually very extroverted, sociable, and well liked. They typically have many friends until they become ill and show symptoms of their reactive depression.

The literature on hysteria is one of the most extensive in psychiatry. Discussions of etiology are numerous. Several authors have differentiated between the mechanisms of psychophysiological reactions and of conversion reactions. Among these authors is Cobb (1950). In contrast to the complicated physiological mechanism involved in psychophysical organ reactions, Cobb points out that the "choice of organ" in conversion hysteria is symbolic and direct and utilizes the voluntary neuromuscular system or the sense organs. Cobb believes that the basic mechanism is the conditioned reflex of Pavlov. Through conditioning, emotional reactions attach themselves to simple and available reflexes such as blushing, vomiting, and urination. This opinion is in accord with that of Meehl (1962) quoted earlier. In Cobb's experience with hysteria, vomiting occurs as the most common symptom, followed by pseudoneurological symptoms of paralysis and sensory loss.

In the discussions of the etiology of conversion reactions, there is generally a heavy emphasis on the importance of learning. Support for this view can be found in data presented by Gottesman (1963). In his MMPI study of identical twins, Gottesman found a low genetic component in the Hs-Hy "conversion hysteria" profiles.

In their summary of research findings on patients with 1-3 MMPI profiles, Dahlstrom and Welsh (1960) note that physical complaints are prominent in the symptom picture. In contrast to patients with 1-2 codes, however, pains more often occur in the head or in the extremities than in the trunk. Pain involving the viscera or bowels is less common than complaints involving the precordium or chest. Complaints of dysfunction of the muscular system or the central nervous system are more frequent than pain in the abdomen. Dahlstrom and Welsh also comment on the high frequency of appetite and eating problems, including anorexia, nausea, vomiting, and overeating.

A comprehensive description of the behavioral characteristics of the hysterical personality is presented by Chodoff and Lyons (1958). These investigators abstracted from the literature the following seven trait clusters upon which authors seem generally agreed:

1.   Egoism, vanity, egocentric, self-centered, self-indulgent.

2.   Exhibitionism, dramatization, lying, exaggeration, play acting, histrionic behavior, mendacity, pseudologica phantastica, dramatic self-display, center of attention, simulation.

3.   Unbridled display of affects, labile affectivity, irrational emotional outbursts, emotional capriciousness, deficient in emotional control, profusion of affects, emotions volatile and labile, excitability, inconsistency of reactions.

4. Emotional shallowness, affects fraudulent and shallow, go through motions of feeling.

5. Lascivious, sexualization of all nonsexual relations, obvious sexual behavior, coquetry, provocative.

6. Sexual frigidity, intense fear of sexuality, failure of sex impulses to develop toward natural goal, sexually immature, sexual apprehensiveness.

7. Demanding, dependent.

These seven clusters provide generally agreed-on criteria on which to base the diagnosis of hysterical personality. Chodoff and Lyons found, however, that only 3 of a group of 17 patients in a VA Hospital who were diagnosed "conversion reaction" showed all seven of the categorical criteria for the hysterical personality. For the patients of the 1-3-2 type in the present study, similar findings would obtain. It should be noted, however, that there is considerable overlap even though few cases would meet all seven of the descriptive criteria.

Dahlstrom and Welsh (1960, p. 172) summarize the personality picture as follows:

> These patients are characteristically lacking in insight, difficult to get motivated in treatment, and, in marked contrast to most psychiatric patients, frequently extroverted and sociable. In a medical setting, these patients are more typically first seen because of their physical complaints and often resist psychological study or any intimation that their difficulties may stem from emotional problems. They find physical or organic explanations more acceptable and compatible with their self-concepts than any psychodynamic causes.

One of the profile types studied by Halbower (1955) carried a 1-3 code. Therapists described these patients as dependent, demanding, selfish, and self-centered. They appeared to be deficient in heterosexual drive. They showed poor self-control, were emotionally labile, and tended to blow up with little provocation. They were not usually considered to be well motivated for intensive psychotherapy.

1-3-7 TYPE

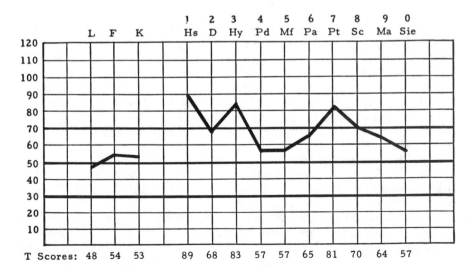

	L	F	K		Hs	D	Hy	Pd	Mf	Pa	Pt	Sc	Ma	Sie
T Scores:	48	54	53		89	68	83	57	57	65	81	70	64	57

Rules

1. Hs, Hy, and Pt highest profile elevations
2. Hs and Hy over T-score 70
3. Pt over T-score 65
4. Hs minus D, 10 or more T-scores
5. K, Pd, and Sie under T-score 70

Mean Profile (N=12)

Diagnosis

Psychoneurosis, anxiety reaction, chronic, with somatization.

Alternative Diagnoses

Mixed neurosis; anxiety hysteria; phobic reaction.

Complaints, Traits, and Symptoms

Anorexia, nausea, vomiting	Headache
Anxiety	Hostile
Cardiac complaint	Insomnia
Depression	Leg or knee pain
Dyspnea, respiratory complaint	Nervousness
Epigastric complaint	Passive
Father punishing	Tension
Fearful	Weak, tired, fatigued
Financial status poor	Wife pregnant or postpregnant

Cardinal Features

Severe anxiety and panic attacks. Phobic about illness. Physiologically unstable and show vascular instability. Persistent clinging and demands for vocational and financial help. Vocational conflict. Trouble settling down into vocational role. Often more interest in hobbies and avocations than in adequate, income-producing job. Unrealistic about work and finances. Complementary marriages (passive-dependent, childish male with attractive, adequate wife). From childhood, predisposed to react to stress with physiological breakdown. Rigid and adapt poorly to environmental changes. Unable to accept aggressiveness in self or others.

DISCUSSION

As would be expected from the prominence of the 1 and 3 elevations in this profile, there is considerable overlap in symptom picture with other 1-3 profiles. These patients typically complain of physical symptoms. Their anxiety-related symptoms include cardiac complaints, epigastric complaints, and nervousness. Patients are described as passive and dependent. The incidence of anxiety, depression, epigastric and respiratory complaints, fearfulness, nervousness, and tension is considerably higher for this code type, however, than for the 1-3-2 type. These symptoms are related to the Scale 7 elevation which carries with it the loading of high anxiety which is so characteristic of these patients.

In the diagnostic nomenclature of the American Psychiatric Association, these patients were most often classified by psychiatrists under the anxiety reaction category. Careful study of the case materials indicates that although the diagnostic category phobic reaction is not uniformly satisfactory, it is most applicable since it was intended to include those cases formerly diagnosed as anxiety hysteria. The *Diagnostic Manual* describes the category phobic reaction as follows (p. 33):

> The anxiety of these patients becomes detached from a specific idea, object, or situation in the daily life and is displaced to some symbolic idea or situation in the form of a specific neurotic fear. The commonly observed forms of phobic reaction include fear of syphilis, dirt, closed places, high places, open places, animals, etc. The patient attempts to control his anxiety by avoiding the phobic object or situation. . . . The term is synonymous with the former term "phobia" and includes some of the cases formerly classified as "anxiety hysteria."

The diagnostic term which probably is actually most accurately descriptive of patients of the 1-3-7 type is "anxiety hysteria."

Frequently, the 1-3-7 patients were the only children or the youngest in the family. The two extremes of being babied and catered to or of being severely rejected, particularly by a punitive, brutal, and/or alcoholic father suggested origins of later fears and disturbed relationships with authority figures. Regressive phenomena in the 1-3-7 patients were shown in persistent clinging. Demands for financial support were made to hospital sources who appeared to represent father figures for these patients. The patients demanded service-connected pensions and direct financial aid for themselves and their families. There frequently was a history of indebtedness before hospitalization, partly because of personal loans which had been obtained. After hospital admission, these patients were very persistent in getting on lists for free canteen books, in demanding money to finance hospital passes, and in complaining about not receiving enough financial assistance from veterans' funds to provide adequately for their families while they were hospitalized.

In their histories, the 1-3-7 patients were characterized by poor vocational adjustment. Often there was underachievement because of failure to utilize high potential in practical pursuits. Often when there was a stable job history, there frequently was vocational dissatisfaction despite the stability. Prior to hospitalization, the 1-3-7 patients were very often either in the process of changing jobs or of contemplating a change, with resulting conflict stemming from rigidity and needs for security. Actual vocational change was frequently the source of major stress which led to hospitalization. Some of these patients had many skills but seemed fixated at a childish level of engaging in hobbies. This was best exemplified by a college graduate patient who had been a sheet metal worker, plumber, project-engineer, and schoolteacher but who decided during hospitalization that he would like to open a hobby store. Among the 1-3-7 patients, there frequently appeared to be more interest in hobbies or avocations than in income-producing jobs. Feelings of job inadequacy were common. Experiences of job dissatisfaction often took the indirect form of feelings of extreme boredom, escapes into daydreams and fantasies during working hours, and feelings of being unable to tolerate inside work. During hospitalization many of these patients demanded that employment be found for them without effort on their part.

Regression was also apparent in marital adjustment. These patients were frequently dependent on a dominant wife to discipline the children and to take responsibility for family finances. Very often they were described as being unrealistic about practical problems, especially financial matters.

Separation anxiety was most clearly illustrated by inability to keep going when wives were pregnant and particularly when wives were due to deliver. Divorces were infrequent among this group of patients; the one patient who had been divorced remarried his ex-wife even after she bore an illegitimate child between the marriages.

Anxiety and panic attacks at the time of hospitalization were very acute. Prior to hospitalization, the 1-3-7 patients tended to be fearful or phobic about illnesses such as poliomyelitis or heart trouble. Generally unstable physiology and especially unstable vascular systems seemed to provide the basis for the phobias. Often these patients would report sensing that their hearts were pounding, causing them to fear that they would die. Limits of tolerance appeared to be narrow. Often these patients were unable to relax and they tolerated physical environmental changes so poorly that they fell ill while starting on a trip or vacation.

Under stress, the 1-3-7 patients were prone to develop psychosomatic illnesses manifested by epigastric, vascular, and migraine symptoms. In some cases, symptoms suggested "physiological regression." Vomiting and nausea were common. Disturbances over the sight of blood reflected their hysteroid personality component.

Somewhat paradoxically, these patients tended to be rigid, stilted, and highly defensive. On the surface, they were tense and tremulous and often they seemed to dramatize their physical discomfort.

In the *Diagnostic Manual* description of the phobic reaction, the current designation for the former category of anxiety hysteria, the mechanism of displacement is strongly emphasized. Most of the writers on this syndrome agree on this emphasis.

The finding in the 1-3-7 cases of a marked regression to a pattern of dependency strivings most typical of a child toward a parent, and most often toward a father, is consistent with the observation by Maslow and Mittelmann (1941, p. 380) concerning regression in the typical psychodynamics of anxiety attacks. They describe the mechanism as follows:

> Revivals of earlier forms of behavior and reactions (regressive phenomena) are often observable in anxiety attacks. The need and desire to obtain reassurance and safety by being fed or completely cared for as by a protective parent are frequent. Such a patient is frequently found to have been particularly anxious as a child, to have had anxiety attacks at an early age and to have expressed his conflicts and tried to obtain parental help by means of them.

Examination of the literature shows considerable disagreement about the proper classification of anxiety reactions, anxiety hysteria, and phobic reactions. Henderson and Gillespie (1946, p. 159) note that Freud distinguished between anxiety neurosis and anxiety hysteria, but are of the opinion that all these cases should be diagnosed as anxiety states because anxiety hysteria is a confusing and incorrect designation. Henderson and Gillespie argue that theoretically the term "hysteria" should be restricted to patients showing a "capacity for conversion of psychic excitation into bodily innervation." They further object to the term, "anxiety hysteria," on the practical ground that "one of the clinically striking points in hysterias is their lack of conscious fear—their 'belle indifference.'" On the other hand, Maslow and Mittelmann present discrete descriptions of anxiety hysteria, anxiety reactions, and hysterical phobic reactions. In describing anxiety hysteria, Maslow and Mittelmann describe symptoms of acute panic and point out that the anxiety attack is frequently precipitated by injuries to self-esteem which symbolize the patient's feelings of helplessness and dependency. They point out that anxiety attacks occur in persons of various personality types but are most frequently found in individuals with elastic, outgoing personalities. This would be consistent with the presence of the Scale 3 elevation in the 1-3-7 profiles. With regard to psychodynamics, Maslow and Mittelmann (1941, p. 378) state that the anxiety attack approximates a catastrophic state in which the expectation is of injury or abandonment. In this connection, it should be noted that Adelaide Johnson et al. (1941), in their study of child phobias, noted a history of poorly resolved dependency relationships between the child and its mother, an acute anxiety attack in the child produced either by organic disease or some external situation and manifested in hysterical and compulsive symptoms. Separation anxiety is induced both by the attitude of the mother and the dependency relationship to her of the child. In this context, it should be strongly emphasized that almost half the 1-3-7 patients had wives who were either pregnant or post partum.

Maslow and Mittelmann (1941) describe many points in common between patients who develop anxiety reactions and patients who develop phobic reactions, but stress the greater role of displacement in the latter reactions. Strong feelings of helplessness occur in the phobic reaction. Furthermore, the purposive aspect of the phobic attack is more evident than in anxiety attacks.

The 1-3-7 profile seems to contain the elements both of anxiety hysteria and the phobic reaction as described by Maslow and Mittelmann and by the *Diagnostic Manual* and would seem to lend support to Henderson and Gillespie's contention that these categories should not be separate. As will be apparent later, however, a distinction must be drawn between two types of personalities who are prone to develop anxiety attacks. Patients who obtain profiles of the 1-3-7 type tend to have personalities of the elastic, hysterical, outgoing variety. Patients who obtain profiles of the 2-7 type, on the other hand, tend to display obsessional traits. In their discussion of hysterical phobia, Maslow and Mittelmann (1941, p. 383) contrast the avoidance behavior of the phobic reaction with that of the obsessional. Both types of patients attempt to cope with certain problems by carefully avoiding them. Maslow and Mittelmann state that in hysterical phobia, the "tendency to systematic and carefully controlled behavior is not as marked as it is in patients with obsessional reactions, but it is definitely present." These authors also make additional distinctions between phobic reactions and other anxiety attacks:

> The purposive aspect of the phobic reaction is stronger than in anxiety attacks. The displacement is strong and the connections between the situation of stress, the hidden impulses, and the subsequent reactions of these impulses

are hidden. The patient's statement of helplessness and appeal for help are likewise stronger.

No directly relevant references to this three-digit profile type were found in the MMPI literature.

1-3-8 (2) TYPE

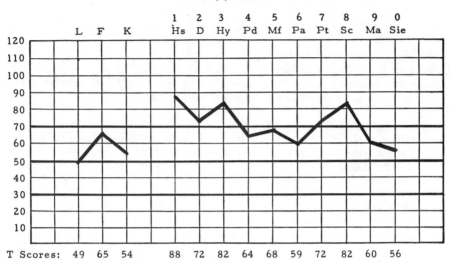

T Scores: 49 65 54 88 72 82 64 68 59 72 82 60 56

Rules

1. Hs, Hy, and Sc highest scales
2. Sc greater than T-score 70
3. Mf greater than T-score 60
4. Pd less than T-score 80

Mean Profile (N=9)

Diagnosis

Schizophrenic reaction, paranoid type.

Alternative Diagnoses

Anxiety reaction in a paranoid personality; schizophrenic reaction, chronic undifferentiated type.

Complaints, Traits, and Symptoms

Agitated	Suicidal preoccupations
Compulsive	(Depression)
Financial status poor	(Heavy drinking)
Religious	

Cardinal Features

Religiosity and religious delusions. Bizarre sexual preoccupation and compulsions. Fears regarding homosexuality. Schizophrenic ambivalence or open hatred, especially toward fathers. Emotionally flat, suspicious, jealous, and paranoid. Develop state of agitation in which they become restless, overbearing, excitable, loud, short-tempered. Demanding. Schizophrenic thinking disturbances and blocking. Denial of psychosexual passivity by masculine occupations such as machinists. Drinking resulting in regressive psychotic behavior. Spells of severe depression and suicidal preoccupation. Somatic symptoms and hypochondriacal concerns that seem to defend against florid outcroppings of schizophrenia.

DISCUSSION

This code represents one type of schizophrenia, a type which can probably best be described as chronic borderline paranoid schizophrenia. In the diagnostic nomenclature, the reaction is best represented by schizophrenic reaction, paranoid type (*Diagnostic Manual*, p. 26):

> This type of reaction is characterized by autistic, unrealistic thinking, with mental content composed chiefly of delusions of persecution, and/or of grandeur, ideas of reference, and often hallucinations. It is often characterized by unpredictable behavior, with a fairly constant attitude of hostility and aggression. Excessive religiosity may be present with or without delusions of persecution. There may be an expansive delusional system of omnipotence, genius, or special ability. The systematized paranoid hypochondriacal states are included in this group.

The 1-3-8 profile type histories contain evidence of pathological families in which parents may have been mentally ill and siblings have shown evidence of poor heredity and/or environment. Siblings frequently were unmarried or died prematurely. Overly close, schizopathic, dependent relationships to mothers were sometimes apparent. Schizophrenic ambivalence was usually present and, in some cases, open hatred for the father was expressed.

Too much sexual concern and naïve attitudes about sex appeared to be related to faulty sexual role learning. Frequently there were homosexual fears or homosexual acting-out. Wives frequently had "female" trouble. Relationships with wives or girlfriends were poor and symptomatic of poor, generally impoverished, schizophrenic-like, interpersonal skills.

The 1-3-8 profile type patients tended to choose masculine occupations such as machinist work or occupations that can support borderline schizophrenics (e.g., railroad switchman or laborer) in spite of intellectual levels which would permit higher strivings. Often these patients had ambitions for higher occupational attainment but broke down if given the opportunity to try to achieve at a higher level.

On admission, these patients frequently showed symptoms of schizophrenic thinking disturbances such as blocking. Somatic symptoms tended to be of a hysteroid kind and suggested physiological instability. Conversion symptoms and hypochondriacal features which apparently defended against florid outbreaks of schizophrenia were common.

Oral fixations were indicated by excessive drinking and dependency with spells of severe depression and suicidal preoccupation. Religiosity and religious delusions were common and seemed to spring from yearnings for strong father figures or power symbols to achieve the integration which was not possible in relation to their own fathers. Although correctly oriented, these patients had acute episodes of bizarre behavior. Frequently, they were emotionally flat, but they could have extreme hostility and/or ambivalence toward other persons. They usually were suspicious, jealous, and paranoid. When agitated, they were described as restless, overbearing, excitable, loud, short-tempered, and pacing. When in better control, they may only have been described as demanding.

These patients showed poor response to treatment and tended to remain chronic borderline schizophrenics.

One of the most highly developed modern conceptualizations of schizophrenia has been provided by Arieti (1959). In discussing the manifest symptomatology of schizophrenia, Arieti describes the emergence of striking anomalies of behavior during the period from puberty until the early thirties. Interest in ordinary life happenings wanes and the patient becomes obsessed, instead, with some specific problems. Finally, he begins to express bizarre ideas and develops ideas of reference and delusions.

All the above symptoms are characteristic of the 1-3-8 patients. Arieti notes that in addition to psychotic thought content, at the beginning of a schizophrenic illness there may be symptoms that seem neurotic, such as asthenia and hypochondriacal complaints. These symptoms are particularly characteristic of the 1-3-8 group and are reflected in the 1-3 component of the profile. Arieti also lists mannerisms, affective disturbances, communication difficulties, loss of abstract ability, and lack of insight as common schizophrenic symptoms.

In addition to the above symptoms, Arieti notes that the paranoid type of schizophrenics tends to have a later onset of psychosis. These patients may assume angry, antagonistic, defiant attitudes. Hallucinations may be absent but ideas of reference and delusions are more common than in other schizophrenics. Arieti observes that progression may be fast and lead to advanced regression in a short time but the paranoid type may regress more slowly than other types and may remain at the first or primary stage. They may be able to do useful work, but suspiciousness, ideas of reference, and delusions may make them antagonistic, rebellious, or even violent. The close correspondence between the findings for the 1-3-8 group and Arieti's description of the paranoid type of schizophrenia supports the impression that they are of this category.

In describing the possible course of schizophrenia, Arieti mentions that there is great variability but that schizophrenia progresses in four stages: a first stage in which reality contact is lost, characteristic symptoms of schizophrenia appear and the patient fights either his illness or the world; a second stage in which the patient accepts his illness and is not bothered by his symptoms; a third stage in which the patient appears to be burned out and adjusts at a primitive level; and a fourth or terminal stage in which behavior is very primitive. The 1-3-8 profile would appear to reflect the first stage of schizophrenic illness.

In discussing the psychodynamics of schizophrenia, Arieti (1959) speaks of schizophrenic psychosis as the "last and most troubled phase of a much troubled life history." He feels that the road to schizophrenia arises from birth or even before. Other writers such as Meehl (1962) place even heavier emphasis on genetics and particularly on defective brain functioning of genetic origin as being fundamental in schizophrenia.

With reference to family dynamics, Arieti describes unhappy families with unhappiness of parents aggravated by their marital interaction. He notes that conflict, tension, and anxiety always existed in schizophrenic families and were both a lifelong destructive agent and a vehicle for the transmission of irrational parental attitudes. Arieti quotes Lidz who found that a frequent marital combination in the parents of schizophrenics was a domineering, nagging, hostile mother who gives the child no chance to assert himself married to a dependent man who is too weak to help the child. Another pattern was a tyrannical father married to a weak mother who gives in. The case histories of the 1-3-8 type frequently reveal overt hatred toward fathers, which suggests greater frequency of the latter parental pattern. The relatively high frequency of masculine occupations (e.g., machinists, laborers, railroad switchmen) also would be more consistent with a background of strong rather than weak fathers.

As was the case with many other three point profile codes, no references specific to the 1-3-8 profile type were found in the MMPI literature.

1-3-9 TYPE

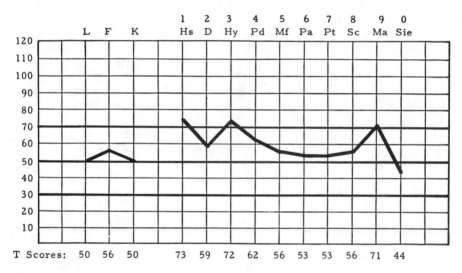

T Scores: 50   56   50   73   59   72   62   56   53   53   56   71   44

Rules

1. Hs, Hy, and Ma highest scale elevations
2. Either Hs, Hy, or Ma greater than T-score 70
3. Hy greater than D by 8 or more T-scores
4. Sie less than T-score 60
5. If Ma greater than T-score 70, Sc 18 or more T-scores less than Ma
6. If Ma less than T-score 70, Sc 7 or more T-scores less than Ma

Mean Profile (N=9)

Diagnosis

Chronic brain syndrome associated with brain trauma and personality disorder.

Alternative Diagnoses

Conversion reaction (with additional organic diagnosis); anxiety reaction.

Complaints, Traits, and Symptoms

Abdominal pain	Headaches	Loss of consciousness
Back pain	Hostile	Numbness
Blindness, eye complaint	Irritable	Tremor
Conflict with wife	Loss of appetite	(Nervousness)

Cardinal Features

Chronic organic illness syndrome, most frequently chronic brain syndrome. If brain syndrome, show temper outbursts. Irritation mounts until patients have "spells" in which they become combative and destructive. Stormy interpersonal relationships. Abnormal EEG records. Somatic complaints of hysteroid type (e.g., back trouble).

DISCUSSION

This profile, like the 2-9 profile reported by Hathaway and Meehl (1951a), seems to be associated, with high frequency, with organic brain dysfunction. (Since the 1-3-9 profile was frequently associated with abnormal EEG findings and/or organic brain damage, organic cases were not excluded in developing this type.) The personality and symptom picture elaborated below for the 1-3-9 patients is strikingly suggestive of the disorders described in the diagnostic categories associated with impairment of brain function. In over two-thirds of these patients, there was definite evidence for brain trauma. Posttraumatic syndromes were most frequently reported, but also included was a pinealoma. Typical symptoms were hearing difficulties, eye complaints, tremor and shaking, and multiple varied somatic complaints. Several patients were taking barbiturate drugs because of their organic illnesses.

The category in the APA *Diagnostic Manual* which best characterizes these patients is that of chronic brain syndrome associated with brain trauma (p. 20):

> Here will be classified the post-traumatic chronic brain disorders, which produce impairment of mental function. Permanent brain damage which produces only neurologic changes because of its focal nature, without significant changes in the areas of sensorium and affect, will not be classified here. Generally, trauma producing a chronic brain syndrome would have to be diffuse and would have to leave permanent brain damage. Post-traumatic personality disorder associated with chronic brain syndrome will be placed in this group with the appropriate qualifying phrase.

This syndrome is classified in the *Diagnostic Manual* as one of the several acute and chronic disorders caused by or associated with impairment of brain tissue function. According to the manual, these disorders are all characterized by a basic syndrome consisting of:

1. Impairment of orientation.
2. Impairment of memory.
3. Impairment of all intellectual functions (comprehension, calculation, knowledge, learning, etc.).
4. Impairment of judgment.
5. Lability and shallowness of affect.

In several of the 1-3-9 cases, parents appeared to be unremarkable and within the normal range of adjustment. In cases in which background data were mentioned, it appeared that most frequently there were problems in relationships with fathers, either because fathers were harsh and rigid, were poor models in the direction of weakness or absence from the home, or because they died during the patient's childhood. The end result of these experiences appeared to be a defect in the ability of these patients to provide a balance between love and authority in their own later attempts to play the roles of husband and father.

The 1-3-9 patients were frequently described as having been highly ambitious prior to military service or to the onset of illness; descriptions suggested overcompensation for feelings of inferiority. Job histories varied. Some patients were described as good workers, particularly in skilled trades, while others had unstable job histories.

The 1-3-9 patients frequently made perfectionistic demands toward their wives and children. They showed little affection toward their families but they showed strong hostility both verbally, in the form of cutting remarks, and physically by choking, assaulting, or being homicidal toward their wives and children, especially when controls were diminished by alcohol. Probably related to these impulses were tendencies to overreact with concern and insecurity when wives became sick or injured themselves even in very minor ways. Divorces were frequent. Relationships with in-laws usually were very stormy.

The major difficulty in adjustment appeared to be associated with temper outbursts. These spells are strikingly similar to the explosive reactions described by Meyer (in Henderson and Gillespie, p. 511) in his classification of the aftereffects of brain injury. In these explosions, to which Kaplan (in Henderson and Gillespie, p. 512) applied the term "explosive diathesis," there is great irritability, especially after alchohol, which sometimes culminates in acts of violence which may seem quite unmotivated, i.e., automatic, or even in an epileptic seizure.

In the 1-3-9 patients, there was generally not enough evidence of impairment of intellectual functioning for it to be emphasized in the histories. This finding, in association with the 1 and 3 scale elevations, is consistent with previous research such as that reported by Friedman (1950). Friedman constructed an MMPI scale which discriminated patients with frontal brain damage from patients with damage in the parietal area. Profiles for the patients with frontal damage were lower in elevation with peaks on Scale 3. Parietal cases showed more elevated profiles with peaks on scales such as 7. Friedman concluded that separation of the frontal and parietal cases was possible because the frontal cases had less manifest disturbance of function and thus were able to react with denial and associated attitudes while parietal cases had more serious disturbances of function and consequently reacted with depression, anxiety, and considerable emotional distress. From this point of view, it would be expected, as was the case, that the 1-3-9 patients would show comparatively little intellectual deterioration and little or no disturbance of sensory motor functions.

In general, it would appear that personality reactions associated with brain trauma are complex and depend on the interaction of previous personality and the preferred defense mechanism with the effects of the brain lesion on functioning. This point of view is amplified in the *Diagnostic Manual* description of the organic syndrome.

According to this description, this syndrome may be the only mental disturbance present or it may be associated with psychotic manifestations, neurotic manifestations, or behavioral disturbance. These associated reactions are not necessarily related in severity to the degree of organic brain disorder or to the degree of brain damage; they are determined by inherent personality patterns, current emotional conflict, the immediate environmental situation, and the setting of interpersonal relations, as well by the precipitating organic disorder. These associated reactions are to be looked upon as being released by the organic brain disorder and superimposed upon it. Since personality function depends greatly on the integrity of brain function, various changes in personality are to be expected with organic brain disorders.

2-7 (3) TYPE

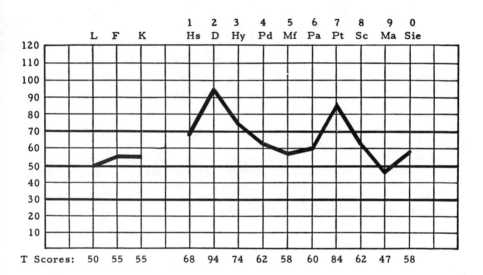

	L	F	K	1 Hs	2 D	3 Hy	4 Pd	5 Mf	6 Pa	7 Pt	8 Sc	9 Ma	0 Sie
T Scores:	50	55	55	68	94	74	62	58	60	84	62	47	58

Rules

1. D and Pt greater than T-score 70
2. D greater than Pt
3. Pt at least 15 T-scores greater than Sc
4. Sie less than T-score 70
5. Pd and Pa less than T-score 80 unless D and/or Pt not greater than T-score 85, in which instance Pd and Pa less than T-score 70

Mean Profile (N=13)

Diagnosis

Psychoneurosis, anxiety reaction.

Alternative Diagnoses

Obsessive-compulsive neurosis; depressive reaction.

Complaints, Traits, and Symptoms

Anorexia, nausea, vomiting	Obsessions
Anxiety	Tension
Cardiac complaint	Weak, tired, fatigued
Depression	Worrying
Nervousness	

Cardinal Features

High standards of performance and achieve well. Capable of emotional ties. Chronically anxious and striving to do well. Vulnerable to accumulated increments of stress from pregnancy of wives, purchases of new houses, illness in families, etc. When unable to tolerate additional anxiety, become depressed, clinging, dependent, self-depreciatory, lose confidence, feel inferior, become overwhelmed. Have somatic manifestations of anxiety (e.g., diarrhea, chest pain, nervous stomach, dizziness, etc.).

DISCUSSION

As would be expected from the high elevation on Scale 7, these patients present symptoms of acute anxiety. The general symptom picture is best characterized in the *Diagnostic Manual* description of anxiety reaction (p. 32):

> In this kind of reaction the anxiety is diffuse and not restricted to definite situations or objects, as in the case of phobic reactions. It is not controlled by any specific psychological defense mechanism as in other psychoneurotic reactions. This reaction is characterized by anxious expectation and frequently associated with somatic symptomatology. The condition is to be differentiated from normal apprehensiveness or fear. The term is synonymous with the former term "anxiety states."

The 2-7 profile type patients also show neurotic personality features of the obsessional reaction type as described by authors such as Maslow and Mittelmann (1941, p. 387). The 2-7 patients combine the psychodynamics of the anxiety states with many of the personality features or characterological traits common in obsessive-compulsive neurosis, but in many instances without the ritualistic symptoms of the obsessive-compulsive as described in the *Diagnostic Manual* (p. 33):

> In this reaction the anxiety is associated with the persistence of unwanted ideas and of repetitive impulses to perform acts which may be considered morbid by the patient. The patient himself may regard his ideas and behavior as unreasonable, but nevertheless is compelled to carry out his rituals.

Background histories for the 2-7 profiles show close correspondence to the observation about etiology of Henderson and Gillespie (1946, p. 161) and the observation about personality traits mentioned by Maslow and Mittelmann (1941). These 2-7 patients frequently come from homes where mothers were anxious and perfectionistic. In the population of veterans, backgrounds were often deprived as a result of such factors as poverty or the death of a parent. High or rigid standards existed in the family, however, and the patients reacted to adversity by becoming responsible and doing their share even at a comparatively early age.

With high standards of performance, these 2-7 patients tended to achieve well, whether in school, in military service, or in vocation. Occupations such as small business operator, clerk, accountant, or those involving manipulative skills (e.g., tool and diemaker or carpenter) tended to predominate in the population of hospitalized veterans.

The 2-7 patients were usually married and their marriages tended to be lasting, stable, and productive of children. These patients are capable of emotional expression. They can be sentimental and can express deep feelings of love. They are also able to display temper, but they often use passive, indirect means for expressing their anger. They hold perfectionistic mothers as ideals and as a result may be critical of their wives; for example, they demand high standards of housekeeping and personal appearance from them. The 2-7 patients are described as good husbands and fathers. They express positive feelings toward their own fathers and identification with them is strong and positive.

Since the 2-7 patients are chronically anxious and striving to do well, they are highly vulnerable to accumulated additional stresses such as pregnancy of wives, responsibilities of a new house, or illness among family members. When they are unable to tolerate these increments to their anxiety, they become depressed and self-depreciatory. They lose confidence, feel inferior, and feel overwhelmed by 'their problems. The high level of responsible behavior which they displayed from an early age may leave them with poorly resolved dependency strivings. When they break down, they may become clinging and regress to a childish level of dependency.

The 2-7 patients usually improve rapidly in the hospital setting. They tend to respond poorly to electroshock therapy, but they show good response to the support of total push programs and they tend to profit from ventilation.

Needed clarification of the etiology of anxiety attacks has been provided by Henderson and Gillespie (1946, p. 161). Their discussion provides a useful background for viewing etiology, which is highly similar to the empirical findings for the 2-7 patients. These authors point out that the origins of anxiety states may be found in all types of conflicts of individual needs with reality. They describe several important etiological factors, including hereditary predispositions to be anxious, an early family environment which included an anxious mother, and a type of personality characterized by a proneness to worry. They list several types of precipitants of anxiety attacks such as financial, business, domestic, or sexual dissatisfaction as well as overwhelming, sudden external stress experiences.

The discussion provided by Maslow and Mittelmann (1941, p. 388), representative of many in the literature, also provides valuable framework for viewing the background data and character traits of the 2-7 patients. These authors list the anal personality traits of orderliness, excessive cleanliness, stubbornness, and stinginess (noted by Freud) plus strong idealistic trends with great conscientiousness and tenderness and considerateness in interpersonal relationships.

Maslow and Mittelmann point out that patients whose dominant symptoms are obsessional reactions are also usually troubled by disturbances in various organic functions such as headaches, difficulties in elimination, disturbances in appetite and eating, and spells of dizziness. The 2-7 patients frequently displayed physical symptoms which appeared to be somatic manifestations of anxiety. These included diarrhea, chest pains, nervous stomach, and dizziness which sometimes verged on blackouts.

Dahlstrom and Welsh (1960, p. 178) report that the 2-7 combination is the most frequent high point pair in hospitalized psychiatric patients. Previous research studies found depression, tension, and nervousness to be the most prominent presenting complaints. Some findings relating to the 2-7 high points might not apply to the present 2-7 profile type since it was narrowly specified to exclude high elevations on scales such as Scale 8. Findings such as those of Guthrie (1949) in which males with 2-7 high points showed rigidity and excessive worrying of the obsessive-compulsive sort would appear to be most relevant.

Halbower (1955) found that 2-7, 7-2 code combinations were second highest in frequency in his VA Mental Hygiene Clinic population. He specified other profile contingencies than just the two high points and found his male sample to be characterized by Q-sorts as intelligent, manifesting feelings of inadequacy, inferiority, and insecurity, and as showing strong achievement needs.

2-7-4 (3) TYPE

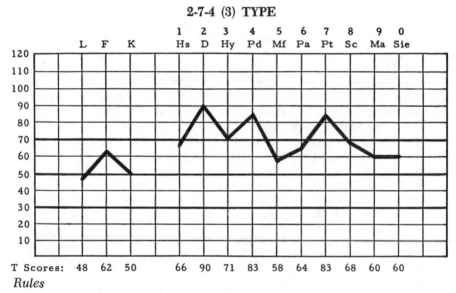

T Scores: 48 62 50   66 90 71 83 58 64 83 68 60 60

Rules

1. D, Pd, and Pt above T-score 70
2. Pt minus Sc at least 5 T-scores
3. Pt minus D 10 T-scores or less
4. D minus Pd 20 T-scores or less
5. Among scales D, Pd, and Pt, two scores below T-score 100
6. If Pd is peak, include only if Pd does not exceed D or Pt by more than 10 T-scores
7. Sie below T-score 70
8. Ma less than Sc
9. Ma above T-score 40
10. If Ma is below T-score 50 include only if Sie does not exceed Ma by more than 15 T-scores.

Mean Profile (N=27)

Diagnosis

Anxiety reaction with alcoholism in passive-aggressive personality.

Alternative Diagnoses

Depressive reaction with alcoholism; passive-aggressive personality with alcoholism.

Complaints, Traits, and Symptoms

Anxiety	Insomnia
Conflict with wife	Tension
Financial status poor	(Depression)
Heavy drinking	

Cardinal Features

Chronic alcoholism which may lead to delirium tremens. Anxious, tense, inferiority feelings, guilt. Severe marital conflict. Dependent on wives and mothers. Passive-aggressive.

DISCUSSION

The high elevation on Scale 4 would be expected to be associated with a high incidence of alcoholism in this profile type, while the elevations on Scales 2 and 7 would predict depression and anxiety. It is interesting to compare this profile type, in which the incidence of heavy drinking was 96 percent, with the 1-2-3-4 profile type which also showed a very high incidence of severe alcoholism. In the latter instance, alcoholism and personality defects appeared to be associated with physiological hyperreactivity of the gastrointestinal tract. In the case of the 2-7-4 profile type, chronic severe alcoholism and personality defects are associated with anxiety, tension, inferiority feelings, and guilt.

The APA *Diagnostic Manual* description of personality trait disturbance has already been given. (See page 28.) The description of the subtype, passive-aggressive personality, is as follows (p. 37):

> The aggressiveness is expressed in these reactions by passive measures, such as pointing, stubbornness, procrastination, inefficiency, and passive obstructionism.

In the backgrounds of the 2-7-4 patients, very frequently there was a history of an extremely close relationship with mothers. This was even more consistent than was the case for the 1-2-3-4 profile type. Frequently, there was mention of a hard-driving, successful father, of much older siblings, or of siblings with whom patients were compared unfavorably.

Often the 2-7-4 patients were described as being afraid to try because of fear of possible failure, a finding common also in the histories of the 1-2-3-7 profile type. The 2-7-4 patients frequently underachieved in academic performance. In vocational performance they were usually described as good workers on a particular job, but because of alcoholism, job histories reflected much instability. There appeared to be dynamic significance in relation to feelings of inferiority in the frequent choice of occupations involving manipulation of power objects. Examples were aircraft and/or automobile mechanics. Saleswork in lines such as shoes, tobacco, or liquor in which positive social stimulus value is an important asset also was frequent. These patients often were described as superficially outgoing, smooth, and needing to be liked. They described in themselves strong feelings of inferiority.

The 2-7-4 patients are usually hostile, dependent, and highly immature. When married, they frequently affect their wives so adversely over the long run that the wives describe themselves as feeling highly nervous or physically ill. Often wives report actually having suffered a nervous breakdown. The marriages are frequently stormy and very often culminate in divorce. Most wives are described as dominating, but wives who are characterized as being immature and "fly-by-night" are also frequent.

Upon hospital admission, anxiety and depression are usually manifest. Strong feelings of guilt are frequently reported. Suicidal thinking is often present and in some cases drinking appears to have a suicidal intent. The severe addiction to alcohol sometimes results in the appearance of delirium tremens at a comparatively young age. Self-defeating tendencies of diverse kinds can be inferred and self-depreciatory attitudes are common at the time of hospitalization.

Poor response is shown to therapeutic measures in the hospital. These patients are frequently described as being unavailable for psychotherapy. In most instances, the only benefit hospitalization has to offer is a period of temporary "drying-out."

In their review of the personality traits of alcoholics, Sutherland et al. (1950) concluded that there was no evidence that persons of one type are more likely to become alcoholics than persons of another type. They suggested that among the methodological errors leading to the negative research findings was the failure to separate alcoholic groups into more homogeneous categories relative to personality characteristics. Inspection of the literature since the time of their review indicates that their conclusion has not been heeded. Almost all psychometric studies have lumped together alcoholics with a variety of character and personality reaction types and have reported mean tests results for heterogeneous samples. The important differences between the 1-2-3-4 profile type and the 2-7-4 profile type in the present study would seem to underscore the importance of the Sutherland et al. observation.

The case histories of the 2-7-4 patients reveal several factors which may have contributed to chronic dependence on alcohol but offer few clues about whether these are necessary or sufficient causes. The possible role of genetics cannot be overlooked. It appeared in the 2-7-4 profile type histories, however, that aside from a possible predisposition to develop tension, anxiety, and fearfulness, which is the case with other profile types containing high elevations on Scale 7, environmental circumstances were the most distinctive differences between the 2-7-4 patients and other profile types.

The only significant finding in past MMPI research which might relate to the 2-7-4 profile type is the previously noted persistent appearance of Scale 4 elevations in diagnosed alcoholics.

2-7-8 (4-0-1-3-5-6) TYPE

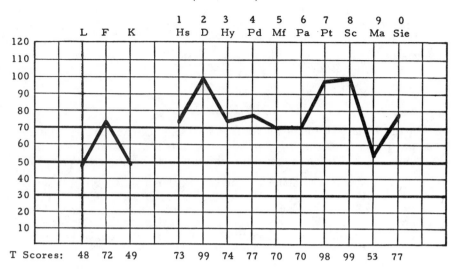

| T Scores: | 48 | 72 | 49 | | 73 | 99 | 74 | 77 | 70 | 70 | 98 | 99 | 53 | 77 |

Rules

1. D, Pt, and Sc over T-score 70
2. D minus Sc less than 15 T-scores
3. Pt and Sc less than 20 T-scores apart (unless D or Pt or Sc greater than T-score 100)
4. If Pt is peak, include only if all other scales below T-score 90 and Pt is not more than 5 T-scores greater than D
5. Sie greater than Ma
6. Ma below T-score 70
7. D minus Hs more than 10 T-scores
8. Pa less than T-score 80

Mean Profile (N=22)

Diagnosis

Pseudoneurotic or chronic undifferentiated schizophrenia.

Alternative Diagnoses

Anxiety reaction or depressive reaction in schizoid personality.

Complaints, Traits, and Symptoms

Blunted or inappropriate affect	Inferiority feelings
Depression	Loss of interest
Difficult concentration	Ruminations
Fearful	Schizoid
Ideas of reference	Weak, tired, fatigued
Inadequacy feelings	Withdrawn, introversive

Cardinal Features

Pseudoneurotic schizophrenics. Ambivalent. Unable to love. Most frequently unmarried. Pan-anxiety, shy, quiet, withdrawn, obsessive, ruminative, sensitive. Thinking may be bizarre. Flat affect. Severe depression, fatigue, weakness, insomnia, apathy. "Perpetual students." Strong feelings of inadequacy and inferiority. Indecisive. Somatic symptoms of anxiety (e.g., heart symptoms, numbness, muscle twitching) and peculiar "neurologic" symptoms involving gross musculature. Interest in reading and ruminating about obscure subjects or religion. Ideas of reference and brief acute psychotic episodes.

DISCUSSION

In the diagnostic nomenclature of the American Psychiatric Association, the patients of the 2-7-8 profile type are best characterized in the description of schizophrenic reaction, chronic undifferentiated type (p. 27):

> The chronic schizophrenic reactions exhibit a mixed symptomatology, and when the reaction cannot be classified in any of the more clearly defined types, it will be placed in this group. Patients presenting definite schizophrenic thought, affect, and behavior beyond that of the schizoid personality, but not classifiable as any other type of schizophrenic reaction, will also be placed in this group. This includes the so-called "latent," "incipient," and "pre-psychotic" schizophrenic reactions.

Although this category affords the best diagnostic grouping available in the current nomenclature for the 2-7-8 type, it represents an example of diagnosis by exclusion and does not provide much insight into the specific nature of the disorder afflicting the 2-7-8 patients. The 2-7-8 patients fit very closely to the description of pseudoneurotic schizophrenia by Hoch and Polatin (1949). Hoch and Polatin's work provides additional insight into the nature of the disorder. It will be discussed in more detail later.

The 2-7-8 patients tend to have a history of poor child-parent relationships. The patterns may vary; sometimes reported is a stern, critical, rejecting father who, although possessing high standards of performance, has achieved only a mediocre status for himself. Sometimes the mother appears to have been overprotective or rejecting. Often rejection appears to have been the indirect result of illness or death of a parent. Poor sibling relationships are frequently noted with reports such as a sibling who was considered to be "superior" or "favored." Also teasing by siblings is of sufficient note to be reported in many cases. Often these patients fall into the middle of the age distribution of siblings. These patients were peculiar in childhood and tended to evoke negative responses from other persons. In the family setting, the presence of pathological qualities in the child may have caused complex interactions with other members of the family who shared the same kind of idiosyncrasies as a result of their common heredity and environment.

Intelligence tends to be above average in these patients, with many reporting successful striving in college and specialized schools. Many of the 2-7-8 patients appear to be of the "perpetual student" type often encountered in college settings. Such overriding traits as indecision, loss of interest, poor interpersonal relationships, and other neurotic-like psychological and somatic symptoms result, however, in poor vocational adjustment. Even when the initial step into the nonacademic world can be taken, there is apt to be much shifting about. Often, despite superior intellect and specialized training, eventual employment is in common laboring occupations.

These patients are almost always lacking in social skills and are particularly inept at developing heterosexual relationships. They often express a need for love but cannot work to develop a relationship which might satisfy this presumed need. Sometimes they attempt to do this in a seemingly easy, parasitic way by becoming attached to married women. Often they have a history of ill-fated heterosexual affairs which culminated in marked disappointment. With high frequency they are single. When married, they are very unsuccessful in the role of husband and are either ambivalent or openly hostile toward their wives. They are sometimes quite perplexed and openly verbalize that they are incapable of love. Frequently included among general feelings of inadequacy are strong fears about lack of masculine adequacy and concern about homosexuality. At least in some cases this is associated with a history of dominance by older sisters as well as by mothers.

Very frequently associated with the history of negatively reinforcing interpersonal experiences are deep-seated feelings of ambivalence which not only characterize relationships to other persons but generalize to all areas of living. In addition, these patients show strong feelings of inadequacy and inferiority. Often there is overconcern about physical appearance, involving such features as slight stature or loss of hair. The 2-7-8 patients are anxious, shy, quiet, and withdrawn. They are fearful and distrustful of other persons and are extremely sensitive to criticisms and opinions of them by others.

Apparently basic to maladjustment is a thinking disturbance which by the time of hospitalization results in thinking being described as bizarre and ruminative despite intact contact with reality. Interests in reading, in studying obscure subjects, or in religion often provide a focus for ruminations. Ideas of reference and brief psychotic episodes may occur, but delusions and hallucinations are most often not present or are fleeting in nature.

Anxiety is pervasive and expressed through anxious thought content, such somatic complaints as heart symptoms, numbness, muscle twitching, and peculiar neurologic-like symptoms involving gross musculature. Severe depression is indicated by suicidal thoughts or suicide attempts, easy fatigue, weakness, insomnia, and apathy. Guilt is excessive, and sometimes restitutive tendencies are expressed by thoughts about doing social service or religious work.

The 2-7-8 patients appear to be classical cases of the disorder which has been termed "pseudoneurotic schizophrenia" by Hoch and Polatin (1949). Other writers have described similar syndromes. For example, Zilboorg (1941) has described "ambulatory schizophrenia" and Federn (1952) has described "latent schizophrenia." Descriptions of these borderline schizophrenic states contain many similarities, but the authors differ in their views of the origins of the disorder, or disorders, and the mechanisms involved.

According to Hoch and Polatin (1949), in order to establish the diagnosis of the pseudoneurotic form of schizophrenia, it is necessary to demonstrate the presence of the basic mechanisms of schizophrenia. The basic mechanisms of schizophrenia are held to differ quantitatively and qualitatively from mechanisms seen in the true psychoneurosis. According to Hoch and Polatin, the diagnosis is based on the constellative evaluation of a group of symptoms, none of which is absolutely characteristic of schizophrenia. These authors believe the basic schizophrenic mechanism to be an autistic and dereistic life approach and maintain that this mechanism has been present "in a subtle way" in all the cases they have observed of pseudoneurotic schizophrenia. Accompanying this mechanism is withdrawal from reality. Ambivalence is another basic mechanism in Hoch and Polatin's view. In pseudoneurotic schizophrenia, in contrast to the neuroses, the ambivalence is not localized but is widespread and diffuse and quantitatively is better described as a "polyvalence" since many constantly shifting notions in the approach to reality are present rather than only two contradictory impulses. Affective disturbance can also be observed in these patients, including inappropriateness, lack of modulation, and lack of flexibility in emotional display.

Hoch and Polatin (1949, p. 250) believe that from a diagnostic point of view, however, the most important presenting symptom of the pseudoneurotic patients is pan-anxiety and pan-neurosis:

> Many of these patients show, in contrast to the usual neurotic, an all-pervading anxiety structure which does not leave any life-approach of the person free from tension. Practically everything the patient experiences influences this anxiety. It is a polymorphous anxiety in the sense that no matter how a person tries to express himself or to side-track an issue, to break through the conflict or to avoid it, anxiety is always manifested. All these attempts, to express, side-track, break through or avoid, are present, usually simultaneously. In connection with this diffuse anxiety, a pan-neurosis is also present. The patients usually do not have one or two different neurotic manifestations, but all symptoms known in neurotic illness are often present at the same time. These patients have tensions and many conversion symptoms in connection with anxiety; gross hysterical, or often vegetative manifestations like poor sleep, anorexia, vomiting and palpitation; and at the same time they will express phobias similar to those observed in anxiety hysteria, such as fear of being killed, or being in open or closed places, or riding in subways. These phobias are often combined with other obsessive-compulsive mechanisms. The patient is dominated by these neurotic manifestations which constantly shift, but are never completely absent. In a good many patients, in addition, depression is present, or a so-called anhedonic state, in which the patient does not derive any pleasure from anything. He tries, at the same time, to force pleasurable experiences but without success.

Hoch and Polatin point out that gross thinking disorders are absent but that subtle disorders of thinking are sometimes, although not always, detectable on psychological tests. Inability to associate freely despite high intelligence and a vague, contradictory account of symptoms with inability to elaborate on them are also described by these authors. Brief psychotic episodes occur in which hypochondriacal ideas, ideas of reference, and feelings of depersonalization are interlocked. Sexual preoccupations and polymorphous perverse sexual manifestations are frequent but they are not openly reported as in frank schizophrenia. Regression is not so conspicuous as in full-fledged schizophrenia. Hoch and Polatin believe that the symptomatology of this syndrome suggests most obviously a quantitative difference between neurosis and psychosis, although qualitative differences are also present.

Related MMPI studies have been reported. Peterson (1954) studied a group of false negative cases of subclinical schizophrenia seen in a VA Mental Hygiene Clinic. These patients had originally been given a diagnosis which did not refer to schizophrenia and were later hospitalized and diagnosed as schizophrenic. They obtained a mean MMPI profile coded 8-7-2 and similar in shape to the 2-7-8 profile type. Peterson stresses the importance of testing with this group of patients because they are often misdiagnosed and are treated as psychoneurotics with poor results.

The response to treatment of the 2-7-8 profile type seems to depend most heavily on the choice of tactics. Response to electroshock therapy is almost always poor. Depression may lift temporarily but then anxiety, fear, and rumination may increase. Most help seems to be forthcoming from supportive psychotherapy. Best results may be achieved by particular kinds of therapists. For example, a well adjusted, older, kindly, understanding, motherly female may be especially effective. The use of re-educative techniques involving recognition of (a) faulty self-attitudes and their origin, and (b) faulty interpersonal relationships and their origin appears to be effective. Direction in helping to provide situations in which relearning can take place and in which positive reinforcement is given for efforts to learn new patterns also appears to be constructive.

The present results of the 2-7-8 profile type serve as cross validation of the earlier study of this profile by Gilberstadt (1952).

4 TYPE

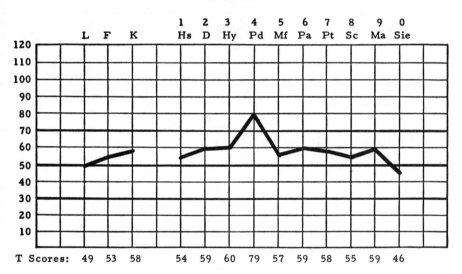

	L	F	K	Hs	D	Hy	Pd	Mf	Pa	Pt	Sc	Ma	Sie
T Scores:	49	53	58	54	59	60	79	57	59	58	55	59	46

Rules
1. Pd greater than T-score 70
2. No other scale as great as T-score 70

Mean Profile (N=17)

Diagnosis

Personality trait disturbance, passive-aggressive personality, aggressive type.

Alternative Diagnoses

Emotionally unstable personality; anxiety reaction; depressive reaction with personality trait disturbance.

Complaints, Traits, and Symptoms

Assaultive	Heavy drinking
Emotional instability	Immature
Financial status poor	(Depression)
Guilt	(Poor work adjustment)

Cardinal Features

Irresponsible, immature, demanding, egocentric, impulsive. Childish, careless, restless, emotionally unstable. Babied by mothers. Divorce infrequent because patients elicit succorant, motherly attitude of forbearance from wives but have severe marital conflict. Sexual maladjustment including perverse sexual behavior and acting-out. Become tense, moody, and depressed because of low frustration tolerance. Suicide attempts, aggressive outbursts toward wives, and alcoholism most frequent causes for admission.

DISCUSSION

The high elevation on Scale 4 in the absence of other elevations in this profile type would predict an active, aggressive, alcoholic, immature type of personality.

The *Diagnostic Manual* of the American Psychiatric Association describes the personality trait disturbance category as follows (p. 36):

> This category applies to individuals who are unable to maintain their emotional equilibrium and independence under minor or major stress because of disturbances in emotional development. Some individuals fall into this group because their personality pattern disturbance is related to fixation and exaggeration of certain character and behavior patterns; others, because their behavior is a regressive reaction due to environmental or endopsychic stress.
>
> This classification will be applied only to cases of personality disorder in which the neurotic features (such as anxiety, conversion, phobia, etc.) are relatively insignificant and the basic personality maldevelopment is the crucial distinguishing factor. Evidence of physical immaturity may or may not be present.

One of the subdivisions under personality trait disturbance in the *Diagnostic Manual* is passive-aggressive personality. Three types are differentiated under this subdivision, one of which, the aggressive type, is described as follows (p. 37):

> A persistent reaction to frustration with irritability, temper tantrums, and destructive behavior is the dominant manifestation. A specific variety of this reaction is a morbid or pathological resentment. A deep dependency is usually evident in such cases. The term does not apply to cases more accurately classified as Antisocial reaction.

More than 50 percent of the patients of the 4 type were described as being overindulged, babied, or overprotected, especially by their mothers. In several instances, the observation that this happened because the child seemed to need such treatment more than other children in the family appeared to suggest a constitutional factor. A history of broken families or of unhappiness because of poor family conditions was noted in about half of the cases. Poor relationships with siblings and rivalry with more successful siblings were also common in the histories for this profile type.

Social histories frequently included sexual maladjustment with a relatively high frequency of perverse sexual behavior and extramarital acting-out. In addition to perverse sexual activity, frequently there were general curiosity about sex and guilt in relation to sexuality.

Severe marital conflict was frequently noted. Wives often worked out of necessity. Furthermore, the patients of the 4 profile type often exhibited a parasitic kind of dependency on their wives. Few of these patients were divorced despite poor marital adjustment, apparently because wives adopted a nurturant, succorant, motherly attitude of sympathy and for-bearance in response to the high degree of immaturity in these patients. The fact that only 17 percent of these patients had not married could perhaps be interpreted as further evidence of strong dependency strivings.

Stable vocational adjustment was reported in about half of the cases, but vocational underachievement could be inferred in many of these cases. The highest achievers were in sales and supervisory positions. The modal 4 patient was employed in a trade or clerical job not requiring highly devel-oped skills or high levels of responsibility. In the area of occupational adjustment, however, patients obtaining profiles of the 4 type seemed to fall more nearly within the range of normal variation than patients with other profile types containing high Pd elevations.

The 4 profile type cases appear to fit closely the description of per-sonality trait disturbance, aggressive type. High frequency trait terms appearing in the case histories of these patients included irresponsible, immature, demanding, egocentric, impulsive, childish, careless, emotionally unstable, and restless. The outstanding trait appears to be low frustration tolerance resulting in assaultiveness. The 4 type patients became depressed, moody, and tense under frustration. They reacted with outbursts of physical aggression, especially toward wives, with suicidal threats, and with alco-holism. They showed evidence of underlying insecurity, guilt, and self-depreciatory attitudes. Frequently, an attempt was made to evade difficult life situations through devices such as alcoholism or lying.

A relatively high frequency of occurrence of this profile type in a sam-ple of neurodermatitis patients (Gilberstadt, 1962) suggests that some 4 type patients may tend to react to frustration with psychosomatic disturb-ances and that physiological immaturity may parallel other types of behav-ioral immaturity in these patients.

In their summary of MMPI research on high-point 4 codes, Dahlstrom and Welsh (1960, p. 188) state:

> Early in the development of MMPI patterns, it was discovered that peak scores on Scale 4, almost without regard to the absolute elevation of the pro-file, provided evidence of lack of social conformity or self-control and a persistent tendency to get into scrapes.

When an attempt is made to tie the 4 type to the literature in psychia-try, a serious difficulty is encountered because the term, "psychopathic personality" has been used so loosely and so overinclusively. Jenkins (1960) has traced the history of the concept of the psychopath. He believes that despite the well-known impreciseness of the term "psychopath," it is a real-istically descriptive term that is based on experience and that will survive. Jenkins characterizes the personality disorder classification into which the psychopathic personality falls as a "stepchild of psychiatry" with a history of reluctant fumbling toward a working definition. He states that the diag-nostic category is unsatisfactory mainly because the diagnosis is reached by exclusion and because it is based on quantitative rather than on qualitative differences from normality. Jenkins argues that the only characteristic that various personality disorders have in common, aside from difficulty in adjustment, is the absence of quantitatively abnormal symptoms.

In Jenkins' view, a distinction should be made between the immature, emotionally unstable, and passive-aggressive personality types and the antisocial classical psychopaths. The latter type will be considered when the data for the 4-9 profile type are presented.

Aichhorn (1935) notes that regularly the childhood of "dissocial" children has been disturbed by a lack of affection or by an undue amount of affection. He feels that satisfactory social adjustment depends on several factors, including adequate constitutional endowment and early love relationships that have been confined within certain limits. Aichhorn observes that the child develops normally and assumes his proper place in society if he can cultivate in the nursery such relationships as can be favorably carried over into the school and from there into the ever-broadening world about him. He feels that every new contact, according to the degree of authority or maturity that the person represents, repeats a previous relationship with little deviation. These observations would appear to be highly relevant to the 4 profile type.

Findings from previous MMPI studies tend to show agreement with findings for the present 4 profile type. Mello and Guthrie (1958) found that self-referred college counselees with peak scores on Scale 4 showed rebelliousness, hostility toward parents, concern about vocational choices, and unstable relationships with the opposite sex. Guthrie (1949) found that medical patients with peak scores on Scale 4 tended to be alcoholic, to gamble excessively, and to show poor work records.

4-3 TYPE

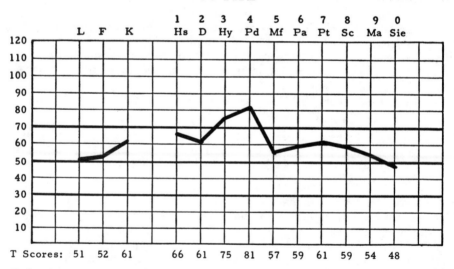

T Scores: 51   52   61   66   61   75   81   57   59   61   59   54   48

Rules

1. Hy and Pd greater than T-score 70
2. No other scale over T-score 70, Hs excepted

Mean Profile (N=17)

Diagnosis

Personality trait disturbance, emotionally unstable personality.

Alternative Diagnoses

Conversion reaction; passive-aggressive personality, aggressive type.

Complaints, Traits, and Symptoms

Assaultive
Father alcoholic
Financial status poor
Headache
Heavy drinking
Hostile

Impulsive
Moodiness
Suicide attempt
(Conflict with wife)
(Depression)

Cardinal Features

Poorly controlled anger resulting in temper outbursts. Sensitivity to rejection or frustration of egocentric demands for attention and approval. Aggression turned outward results in aggressive outbursts in which homicidal threats are made or attempts are made to choke wives, children, or others. Aggression turned inward results in suicide attempts. High rate of suicide attempts (40 percent). Unsuccessful in roles of husband or father. Life role in which patient is most likely to succeed is work as salesman. Somatic symptoms of headache, blackout, eye complaints. Alcoholism most frequent single symptom. May show symptoms of conversion reaction.

DISCUSSION

The term "emotional instability reaction" is synonymous with the former diagnosis of psychopathic personality, emotional instability. The *Diagnostic Manual* of the American Psychiatric Association lists the term under the category of personality trait disturbance. In contrast to the persistent reaction to frustration with irritability, temper tantrums, and destructive behavior previously noted to be characteristic of the passive-aggressive personality, aggressive type (and presumably the 4 profile type), the emotionally unstable personality is described as follows (p. 36):

> In such cases the individual reacts with excitability and ineffectiveness when confronted by minor stress. His judgment may be undependable under stress, and his relationship to other people is continuously fraught with fluctuating emotional attitudes, because of strong and poorly controlled hostility, guilt, and anxiety.

This description would appear to parallel closely the findings for the 4-3 profile type.

There is obviously much overlap between the findings for the 4 and the 4-3 profile type. Check-list differences which appear to be most significant are the greater incidence for the 4-3 type of somatic complaints, of deprivations in relation to fathers, and of suicide attempts. The modal picture for the 4-3 profile type was one of severe rejection by fathers and, in some cases, actual desertion. Items seemingly of significance which were more frequent for the 4 profile type as compared to the 4-3 type were crying, assaultiveness, guilt, and disturbed mothers.

The sensitivity to rejection and lack of approval apparently stemmed from the severe rejection in early childhood. Eighty percent of the patients had fathers who were described in various strongly negative terms. In a few cases, parental overindulgence was reported, but most fathers were described as either brutally sadistic, overtly rejecting, alcoholic, family deserters or as absent because of death. In a few cases, mothers were also described as lacking affection.

In some cases, truancy, expulsion, and general rebellion toward school were reported, but in others relatively good school adjustment apparently related to social outgoingness was noted.

Educational histories varied. In several instances, difficulties in deportment terminated high school attendance. There was a high incidence of dropouts among 4-3 type patients who attended college or vocational schools. Employment tended to be in various semiskilled occupations. Vocational maladjustment and poor job identification were frequent. A major and striking exception to the generally poor performance in vocational roles was shown by the comparatively large proportion of these patients who succeeded in the field of sales. Several of the 4-3 patients were described as smooth, suave, polished salesmen. The marked contrast between this aspect of the social histories and the remainder of the material suggested that this tended to be one of the few major life roles in which 4-3 patients might be expected to succeed or to excel.

Marital adjustment tended to be very poor. A history of marked marital discord occurred in almost all cases. In many cases there were several unsuccessful tries at marriage. Divorce and threatened divorce were frequent. Often, the 4-3 patients complained about a lack of sympathy and understanding from their wives. Marital disturbances frequently were precursors of suicide attempts. The poor aptitude for marriage appeared to be symptomatic of general inability to play adult roles whether of husband, father, or responsible citizen.

The most outstanding trait of the 4-3 profile type was poorly controlled anger which resulted in temper tantrums, most frequently associated with sensitivity to rejection but also frequently associated with inability to tolerate the frustration of immature, egocentric demands for attention and approval. When turned outward, the expression of anger frequently took the form of aggressive outbursts in which patients attempted to choke wives or children and made homicidal threats. When turned inward, anger took the form of impulsive suicidal attempts. The latter occurred in about 40 percent of the cases. In the hospital, these patients were described as excitable, sullen, and moody. Somatic symptoms such as headaches, blackouts, or eye symptoms were most frequent.

The writers on psychopathic or personality trait disturbance types quite uniformly express dissatisfaction and confusion about the finer diagnostic breakdowns of these patients. Most writers agree that emotional instability is very frequently a trait in various kinds of immature personalities, but the authorities seem to be unable to formulate clearly the unique symptoms, traits, and psychopathology of the specific categories in a way which is generally accepted.

In relation to the general category of psychopathic personality, Preu (1944, p. 924) has made this statement:

> The diagnosis has never been made dependent on the recognition of particular symptoms or kinds of behavior in the direct descriptive sense, nor on the demonstration of the operation of particular behavioral dynamics, nor on the demonstration of the existence of any definite etiologic factor. The emphasis has been predominantly but not exclusively on the occurrence of social maladjustment, particularly on the occurrence of persistent social maladjustment in the absence of the symptoms of the traditional clinical entities of psychiatry.

Preu states that the diagnosis of psychopathic personality is established if (a) outward social maladjustment is brought to the attention of a psychiatrist, (b) the maladjustment is continuous or repeatedly recurrent, and (c) the difficulty in adjustment clearly is not due to defective intelligence, structural brain disorder, epilepsy, neurosis, manic-depressive psychosis, or schizophrenia.

Preu points out that a diagnosis based on these three criteria is made by exclusion. The chief symptoms of psychopathy are indications of maladjustment such as delinquency and law-breaking, socially unconventional behavior which interferes with adjustment, aberrant sexual behavior, drug addiction and chronic alcoholism, and emotional instability. The latter symptom appears to be most characteristic of the 4-3 profile type. Preu (1944, p. 925) describes this area of difficulty as follows:

> Emotional instability and other affective liabilities to comfortable social adjustment also constitute a widely accepted basis for the symptomatic diagnosis of psychopathy. Emotional instability is understood to include emotional lability in general and conspicuous excitability in particular as shown by the occurrence of poorly controlled and more or less unpredictable emotional outbursts, especially with irritability and aggressiveness. The individual with such symptoms is sometimes referred to as an epileptoid psychopath. Other affective symptoms of psychopathy include habitual gloomy mood and the occurrence of frequent swings of mood in the direction of depression or elation, the latter characterizing the cycloid psychopath. It is not clear at what point the distinction is to be made between psychopathic mood swings and manic-depressive attacks.

Another writer on the concept of psychopathic personality, Freyhan (1955, p. 239), has stated:

> The concept of psychopathic personality concerns individuals with characterological abnormalities. These abnormalities do not constitute a nosological entity; one cannot reduce them to single formulas of characterization, but one must evaluate them from the point of view of individuality.

Freyhan describes the *symptomatic approach* to the concept of psychopathic personality in which types of psychopathic conduct are described in relation to prominent clinical symptoms such as impulsiveness, eccentricity, or emotional instability. The approach is exemplified by writers such as Schneider (in Freyhan, 1955), who grouped psychopathic personalities into ten types based on his clinical studies. Secondly, Freyhan describes the *etiologic approach* involving "fundamental concepts of personality." As an example of the etiologic approach, he discusses the formulation of Kahn (1931), who employed the term "developmental anachronism" to stress that psychopaths differ quantitatively and not qualitatively from normal persons. (As noted previously, recent writers on psychopathy such as Jenkins have reiterated this point of view.)

Kahn (1931) posited three main structural aspects of personality: (1) impulse, or "an animal vital urge toward an ultimately biological satisfaction of a need," which is manifested in drive and energy output; (2) temperament, which "comprises mood and affect and transforms the impulses and which includes fundamental mood or characteristic feeling tone and reactive emotionality"; and (3) character which is defined as "the directedness of the personality or the steerage toward a definite goal." Kahn grouped psychopathic personalities by the abnormalities of interrelation-ships between impulse, temperament, and character. In the context of Kahn's theory, the 4-3 profile type would show particular imbalance of temperament.

Previous research with MMPI 3-4 and 4-3 profile codes has been reported. In the present population, at an earlier date, Welsh and Sullivan (Dahlstrom and Welsh, 1960, p. 190) found the psychiatric diagnosis, pas-sive-aggressive personality, passive type, to predominate in cases where Scale 3 was higher than Scale 4.

Guthrie (1949) found problems with impulse control in patients with 3-4 profiles seeking medical treatment. In accord with the present findings for the 4-3 profile type, he found marital difficulty and divorce to be typical. When the code was 4-3 rather than 3-4, Welsh and Sullivan found chronic hostility and aggressive feelings and Guthrie found alcoholism, marital dis-harmony, and sexual promiscuity. All these traits are consistent with present findings for the 4-3 profile type, as is Guthrie's finding of acting-out alter-nating with hysterical kinds of physical illness in some patients.

4-9 TYPE

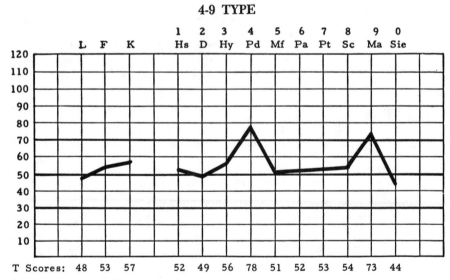

T Scores: 48   53   57   52   49   56   78   51   52   53   54   73   44

Rules

1. Pd and Ma greater than T-score 70
2. No other scale greater than T-score 70
3. L less than T-score 60
4. Ma 15 or more T-scores greater than Sc
5. Pd 7 or more T-scores greater than Mf

Mean Profile (N=10)

Diagnosis

   Sociopathic personality disturbance, antisocial reaction.

Alternative Diagnosis

   Emotionally unstable personality.

Complaints, Traits, and Symptoms

Financial status poor   (Conflict with wife)
Heavy drinking   (Poor work adjustment)
Hostile   (Tension)
Irritable

Cardinal Features

Immature, hostile, rebellious. Poorly socialized, poor morals, poor standards. Impulsive, restless, low frustration tolerance. Superficially friendly, outgoing, and likeable but also self-centered, grandiose, haughty, and hostile. Get moody, irritable. Drinking can result in circumscribed paranoid psychotic episodes. Impulsive suicide attempts. Lack respect for authority. No affection for adults but like children. Become panicky when they realize they are unable to find cultural or emotional ties because of being emotionally crippled. Poor work and marital adjustment. "Psychopathic" occupations.

DISCUSSION

As has been noted previously, the 4-9 profile type appears to correspond most closely to the diagnostic category of sociopathic personality disturbance, antisocial reaction. The APA *Diagnostic Manual* mentions that individuals to be placed in the category of sociopathic personality disturbance are ill primarily in terms of society and of conformity with the prevailing cultural milieu, and not only in terms of interpersonal relations. The *Manual* also states that sociopathic reactions may be symptomatic of severe underlying pathology. The specific category antisocial reaction is described as follows (p. 38):

> This term refers to chronically antisocial individuals who are always in trouble, profiting neither from experience nor punishment, and maintaining no real loyalties to any person, group, or code. They are frequently callous and hedonistic, showing marked emotional immaturity, with lack of sense of responsibility, lack of judgment, and an ability to rationalize their behavior so that it appears warranted, reasonable, and justified. The term includes cases previously classified as "constitutional psychopathic state" and "psychopathic personality." As defined here the term is more limited, as well as more specific in its application.

The 4-9 profile type patients were described as immature, hostile, rebellious, impulsive, and restless. Poor morals and standards were described. Low frustration tolerance resulted in acting-out. Psychosomatic reaction to frustration with ulcers was frequently observed. Superficially, these patients appeared to be friendly, outgoing, and likeable but they were also grandiose and haughty. Heavy drinking was very frequent and was sometimes followed by spells of agitation which reached the degree of paranoid psychotic episodes. Moodiness and irritability were frequent. Depression often appeared on the surface but usually subsided soon after hospital admission.

The modal 4-9 patient was described as having been a child of athletic build who was generally precocious in early development. He was doted upon by others, most frequently his mother, and apparently was thus stimulated to heightened ego development. Frequently, these mothers were described as being critical, unaffectionate, controlling persons who depreciated their husbands. In the 4-9 type, it appeared that, compared to other profile types, such as the 4-3 type for example, there was a much greater frequency of two functioning parents and a much lesser frequency of broken homes but with the presence of a mother who in a subversive way undermined the role of her husband as a father. These mothers frequently appeared to invest much of their stake in life, including strivings ordinarily shared with husbands, in the patients during childhood. Fathers were often deprecated in spite of comparatively high vocational attainment. At least in some cases, it appeared that loose ties with their families were associated with heavy investment of energy in interests outside the home and family (such as in business pursuits) which could be interpreted as reflecting rejection. In instances where fathers were obviously unsuccessful in life attainment, the wives tended to use this as a focus for their scorn. In either case, the effect on the child was to instill a deep-seated disdain and lack of respect for fathers and for authority figures who symbolized parental control.

Although presumably modal, the foregoing dynamics did not appear in all the 4-9 profile type cases. At least one case appeared to have been impulsive and mischievous from early childhood.

In many cases it appeared as if ego development was enhanced until adolescence when decisive turning points frequently occurred. In reviewing several histories, it seemed apparent that social learning had been faulty because of a lack of needed balanced love-authority experiences. Frequently, in these cases there was mention of shyness and inferiority feelings in adolescent heterosexual relationships. This appeared to be symptomatic of defective psychosexual development and of characterological inability to form loving relationships, stemming, in part, from the combination of a controlling mother lacking in emotional warmth and a father who for several reasons was a poor identification model.

The low frustration tolerance, constitutionally determined aggressiveness or impulsive tendencies aside, seemed possibly related to excessive approval from mothers and to easy successes in achievement. Many of the 4-9 profile type patients showed good achievement in school or college. Many were outstanding achievers until a turning point occurred. One patient was a valedictorian, another was a "model boy," and a third completed medical school. Starting in adolescence, and on until early adulthood, decisive conflicts with authority or ego-deflating failures in competitive strivings could precipitate a maladaptive, seemingly almost irreversible course. In some cases, sudden attempts to provide authority and discipline by previously weak or distant authority figures seemed to unleash a strong reservoir of contempt and lack of respect for authority that had been previously inculcated. After the turning point, these individuals who were to become 4-9 profile type patients showed a downhill course. They were highly unstable in job histories and worked in low status or unstable occupations such as laborers, fly-by-night radio announcers, and cab drivers. They also had large intervals of unemployment.

Further along the one-way downhill trail, these patients appeared to become lonely and occasionally perplexed to the point of panic about their inability to relate meaningfully to other persons. Apparently absurd aggressive behavior, strange liaisons with other persons such as prostitutes, and other bizarre activities seemed to represent a frantic, active search for some style of life that would fit their aggressive but emotionally crippled natures. Marriages were always unhappy. Jealousy and hostility toward wives or girlfriends seemed to be symptomatic of inability to love or relate with positive emotions. Positive affection could be directed only toward children, perhaps as a result of some kind of narcissistic identification related to their own childhood experiences. Periodic incarcerations in mental institutions or jails appeared to represent a kind of affiliation, however unproductive in nature, with cultural institutions of a kind which yield strong measures of authority and dependency gratifications of a more or less impersonal kind.

Aichhorn (1935) describes two types of delinquency—one caused by "excess of love" and the other by "excess of severity." The 4-9 profile type cases most frequently seemed to correspond to the former. Aichhorn mentioned that frequently these were only children and noted that the indulgence of the child most frequently occurred in mothers who felt that they received too little love from their husbands. He said (p. 200), "In some instances this feeling may be justified; in others it may arise from an excessive need for love which cannot be satisfied in a normal way." Similar observations, apparently independently arrived at, were reported by Cleckley (1955). In several of the 4-9 profile type cases this type of mother was apparent, as was noted above.

Aichhorn states that delinquency develops because the mother, or in some instances the father, is not equal to the task of rearing the child. He states (1935, p. 201):

> Since such a mother is ready to do anything to keep her darling from suffering the slightest discomfort, she is unable to subject him to any denials. Punishment upsets her more than it does the child. Weighted down by cares for him, she worries continually about his welfare and cannot demand from him any postponement or renunciation of pleasure. She clears out of his way all disappointments and obstacles which the child must learn to face and overcome in later life and thus she robs the child of initiative. His moods are endured with inexhaustible patience, and his naughtiness is admired as an indication of unusual individuality. Any criticism of him is as painful as a personal insult.
>
> This child is the centre of interest and lives without restraint according to the wishes of his pleasure ego. Reality does not exist for him because his mother shuts it out. Since he is unable to modify the pleasure principle, reality is pushed further and further away.... Finally the child makes demands which the mother cannot meet. He can no longer be kept away from reality and when he has to meet it suddenly, he is unprepared for the force of its demands. This encounter either leads to neurosis or it kindles a rebellion which is beyond the control of the parents and which finds expression in all kinds of dissocial acts.

There appears to be a close correspondence between many elements of the above characterization and elements of the histories of many of the 4-9 profile type patients.

Aichhorn also describes the difficulty in treating patients of a "highly narcissistic type." He describes a 17 year old boy who had been a successful stock market speculator and bootlegger at a very young age. He frequented night clubs, gambled, and associated with undesirable persons. His widowed mother sought treatment for him because he began pawning her clothes to obtain money when his funds ran out. Aichhorn says (p. 139):

He was one of those boys who gave no apparent trouble in an institution. Such youths are polite and obliging, handy and useful in simple office work. They know how to get along with others and soon achieve the role of gang leader. When one works more intensively with them, one learns to see their difficulties. Inwardly demoralized but outwardly as smooth as glass, they offer no point of attack. Their behavior is a mask, but a very good one. They show no interest in the personnel, and ward off every attempt to establish a real relationship to them. Thus the transference, which must of necessity be very strongly positive if one is to accomplish anything with them educationally, is almost impossible to establish. In the institution they give the impression of being cured very speedily but when at large again they revert to their old behavior. We must use the greatest caution with them.

These remarks of Aichhorn apply very directly to the 4-9 profile type.

One factor, possibly important etiologically in the development of an antisocial pattern, which seems to be underemphasized by most writers but which is clearly apparent in the 4-9 profile type, is the presence of temperament of an active, aggressive type. Jenkins (1960), in pointing out the great differences between the professional criminal, or *dissocial reaction* type, and the classical psychopath, or *antisocial reaction* type, asserts that the two groups are clearly differentiable in early childhood. By studying the intercorrelations of traits in a very large number of child guidance clinic cases, he found a strong cluster which he called the Syndrome of Socialized Delinquency, consisting of stealing, truancy, police arrest, staying out late at night, and associating with bad companions. This syndrome was characteristic of the budding criminal or dissocial personality that was a cultural product. The second strong trait cluster was called the Syndrome of Unsocialized Aggressive Behavior and consisted, in boys, of disturbing influence in school, violence, fighting, quarrelsomeness, destructiveness, and incorrigibility. (It would appear that this trait cluster could predominate only in children who were of aggressive, active temperaments.) For the sake of contrast, Jenkins presents a third pronounced cluster which he calls the Syndrome of Internal Conflict in boys in which the traits of "sensitiveness over specific fact," inferiority feelings, depressed or discouraged attitude, worry over specific fact, mental conflict, and unhappy manner predominate.

Hathaway and Monachesi (1953) have shown in MMPI research with adolescents that elevations on Scales 4 and 9 are positively related to delinquency while Scales 2, 5 and 7, characteristic of neurotic adults, seem to be associated with inhibition of delinquent behavior. These findings would appear to correspond to the Jenkins trait clusters of Unsocialized Aggressive Behavior, and of Internal Conflict, respectively.

Jenkins cites McCord and McCord (1956) who reviewed the literature and concluded that the two traits of guiltlessness and lovelessness conspicuously differentiate the psychopath.

Jenkins also cites Cleckley's (1955) widely known list of distinguishing psychopathic traits:

1. Superficial charm and good "intelligence."
2. Absence of delusions and other signs of irrational "thinking."
3. Absence of "nervousness" or psychoneurotic manifestations.
4. Unreliability.
5. Untruthfulness and insincerity.
6. Lack of remorse or shame.
7. Inadequately motivated antisocial behavior.

8. Poor judgment and failure to learn by experience.
9. Pathologic egocentricity and incapacity for love.
10. General poverty in major affective reactions.
11. Specific loss of insight.
12. Unresponsiveness in general interpersonal relations.
13. Fantastic and uninviting behavior, with drink and sometimes without.
14. Suicide rarely carried out.
15. Sex life impersonal, trivial and poorly integrated.
16. Failure to follow any life plan.

Jenkins reports a study of 54 psychopathic, or antisocial, veterans who were contrasted with a large psychoneurotic group on a series of background factors. Among the hypotheses that were supported as being antecedents to psychopathic behavior were rejection by father, more than average maternal discipline, negative attitude toward mother, religion no great influence in home, a history of overt sibling rivalry, and a history of marked parental conflict.

Previous MMPI research (Dahlstrom and Welsh, 1960, p. 192) with a 4-9 or 9-4 profile pattern can be summarized as showing overactiveness, acting-out behavior and, in general, aggressiveness and an absence of neurotic disorders in individuals obtaining these profiles.

7-8 (2-1-3-4) TYPE

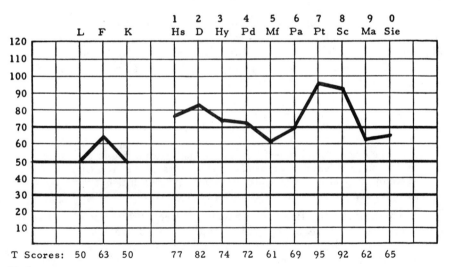

T Scores: 50 63 50   77 82 74 72 61 69 95 92 62 65

Rules

1. Pt and Sc greater than T-score 70
2. Pt and Sc highest scales
3. Pt and Sc less than 10 T-score difference

Mean Profile (N=9)

Diagnosis

Psychoneurosis, obsessive-compulsive reaction.

Alternative Diagnoses

Psychoneurosis, anxiety reaction in schizoid personality with somatization; latent, or chronic borderline, schizophrenia.

Complaints, Traits, and Symptoms

Difficult concentration	Worrying
Father strict	(Depression)
Inferiority feelings	(Nervousness)
Tension	

Cardinal Features

Shy, inadequacy feelings, fearful, lacking confidence, difficulties in interpersonal and heterosexual relationships, sex guilt, poor sexual performance. Frequent forced marriages. Assertiveness and stubbornness in early adult years cover up lack of underlying strength. Dominated by father, older brothers (less frequently by mothers) with resulting dependency-independency conflicts. "Baby" of family. Masculinely identified but feel inferior. Conscientious but achievement mediocre or poor. Major conflicts about job conditions or supervisors because of "adolescent" idealism. Guilt about lack of achievement. Role and sexual problems in marriage. Physiological symptoms of anxiety, especially gastric disturbances. Drink to relax.

DISCUSSION

The elevations on Scales 7 and 8 carry with them anxiety and obsessional, ruminative, ambivalent thinking. In the absence of anhedonia, indicated by the comparatively low elevation on Scale 2 (especially in contrast to the high 2 elevation in the 2-7-8 pseudoneurotic schizophrenic profile type), the profile suggests an obsessional kind of neurotic syndrome.

The *Diagnostic Manual* category which would most closely fit is obsessive-compulsive reaction (p. 33):

> In this reaction, the anxiety is associated with the persistence of unwanted ideas and of repetitive impulses to perform acts which may be considered morbid by the patient. The patient himself may regard his ideas and behavior as unreasonable, but nevertheless is compelled to carry out his rituals.
>
> The diagnosis will specify the symptomatic expression of such reactions, as touching, counting, ceremonials, hand-washing, or recurring thoughts (accompanied often by a compulsion to repetitive action). This category includes many cases formerly classified as "psychasthenia."

Early histories in these patients were frequently characterized by domination by fathers or by older brothers. Less frequently, mothers dominated. In several instances, mothers were described as somewhat rejecting and there was a hint that inherent anxiety, fearfulness, and shyness may have played a strong part in eliciting dominating and rejecting attitudes from other family members. In addition, traits such as food finickiness, stammering, temper tantrums, and enuresis contributed to feelings of inferiority and caused unfavorable comparisons with siblings. Dependence on fathers and older brothers frequently carried over into early adulthood. Many of the 7-8 profile type patients worked in the businesses of their fathers or older brothers. Particularly if this were the case, there tended to be strong dependency-independency conflicts and feelings that they were being "treated like babies" by other family members. Even though the domination and aggressiveness of fathers and brothers usually was resented, the 7-8 patients appeared to retain a strong masculine identification despite strong feelings of inadequacy in relation to masculine roles.

Although these patients were usually described as being highly conscientious, school achievement appeared to be mediocre and several patients failed to complete high school. Difficulty in concentrating, along with shyness, inferiority feelings, and anxiety, seem to be likely surface explanations for the poor performance. After school, occupations tended to be in trades such as watchmaking or printing, in sales, or in laboring jobs. In many cases it seemed likely that occupations were chosen which did not require sustained intellectual concentration. On the job, these patients tended to be conscientious, diligent workers but very frequently there was job dissatisfaction based on adolescent kinds of idealism, conflicts about job conditions, dissatisfaction with supervisors, and dissatisfaction with vocational achievement.

The 7-8 profile type patients showed the frequent psychasthenic traits of guilt, feelings of inferiority, fearfulness, feelings of inadequacy, lack of confidence, conscientiousness and, particularly, attacks of anxiety, tension, and depression when faced with life stresses, especially in the major areas of vocational and marital adjustment. Physiological symptoms tended to be those related to anxiety such as headaches, palpitation, back pain, chest pain, and hypertension. These patients frequently drank excessively in a deliberate effort to relax. Shyness and difficulty in concentrating suggested a schizoid element.

Serious difficulties were apparent in efforts to play adult roles but often this was in contrast to a history of having performed well at an earlier time. Successful performance frequently occurred during military service where a structured, masculine environment not requiring heterosexual adjustment prevailed.

Shyness, feelings of inadequacy and inferiority, and generally poor ability to relate heterosexually were apparent. After marriage, sex guilt and poor sexual performance were still common. Several of these patients entered into marriages forced because of pregnancy which they resented and blamed on their wives. Despite this, in some instances there were several more children born in short succession. (These seemingly paradoxical findings are consistent with Rado's formulations to be discussed below.) During marriage, and particularly in the early years, the 7-8 patients attempted to assert themselves by acting superficially dominant and stubborn but with a lack of underlying strength in these attitudes. Marriages usually were conflictual and unhappy.

In describing reactions in which obsessions and compulsions predominate, Maslow and Mittelmann (1941, p. 388) report:

> A strong idealistic trend with great conscientiousness and tenderness and considerateness toward almost everyone. These features also are fully approved of, and they have very useful social aspects, but they are carried to extremes in patients. The patient may expect himself and others to be motivated only by idealistic impulses, never to become angry but always to settle everything by reasoning, always to treat everyone considerately, and always to understand and forgive. His emotional reactions may be quite definite and outgoing, but usually there is also considerable emotional rigidity.

A very incisive and comprehensive discussion of "obsessive behavior or so-called obsessive-compulsive neurosis" is provided by Rado (1959). Rado points out that difficulties in translation unfortunately resulted in the substitutions in American literature of the term, obsessive-compulsive, for what should have been translated as "obsessional neurosis" and is termed "obsessive behavior" by him. This comment would seem to be germane to the 7-8 profile type who showed little evidence of compulsive symptoms.

Rado distinguishes between obsessive attacks and obsessive traits. The attacks consist of spells of doubting and brooding, bouts of ritual making, and fits of "horrific temptation." Obsessive traits consist of overconscientiousness, of being highly opinionated and proud of intelligence, in having a keen sense of reality, in showing "unswerving integrity," in being perfectionistic, in being sensitive to own hurts, in capability for being destructive, critical, spiteful and vindictive, in being given to bitter irony, in bearing grudges in trivial matters and in being ambivalent, tense, and irritable.

Rado says (1959, p. 338), in his unique terminology, that obsessive behavior is based on a predisposition which is acquired in childhood and includes five "clearly discernible" factors: (1) overstrong rage; (2) guilty fear made stronger by the retroflexion of the larger part of repressed rage; (3) stronger-than-average residues of primordial omnipotence that make rage strong and its paradoxical retroflexion possible; (4) relative pleasure deficiency in the area of genital orgasm, with its consequent enfeeblement of genital love and affection—a deficiency that makes it imperative to control repressed rage by retroflexion; (5) intelligent foresight leading to realistic fears. In addition, Rado says that, presumably, the acquired predisposition to obsessive behavior is based on a genetic predisposition in which the overstrength of rage may be linked with the pleasure deficiency of sexual orgasm. Rado (1959, p. 338) elaborates as follows:

> Parental punishment initiates a pathological development of conscience-repression of defiant rage, first by fear of punishment contingent upon detection, and, later, by fear of conscience of inescapable punishment and guilty fear. The child's fear that the parents can make his omnipotence work in reverse increases his fear of conscience and guilty fear to such a degree that they become capable of retroflexing, as an added safety measure, the larger part of his repressed rage. Retroflexed rage makes remorseful self-reproaches and expiatory self-punishments all the more severe.

These hypothesized dynamics would appear to explain many of the traits found for the 7-8 profile type in a highly consistent fashion.

In addition, Rado's theories about "sexual pain dependence" of the obsessive patient appears to be a highly probable explanation for the unusual finding of a combination of forced marriages, poor sexual adjustment, and multiple children despite marital dissatisfaction in many of the 7-8 profile type patients. Rado (1959, p. 338) states:

> As a source of pleasure, genital orgasm is unrivaled. If, as they usually do, the parents interfere, the organism puts up a hard fight to protect it. We have already seen that the child may circumvent the parental prohibition by indirect modes of stimulation. But there are other methods. Defeated as a child by the campaign of deterrence, the adolescent may find himself inca-pacitated for standard sexual performance. By chance, he then discovers that his submission to humiliation or other abuse has a disinhibitory effect upon his performance. Analysis reveals the reason: He has taken the inescapable punishment beforehand; now he is entitled to prove that he deserved it. He develops the practice of inviting abuse (short of serious injury) from the mate, thereby restoring his (her) capacity for performance. We call this practice the fear-ridden or submissive version of sexual pain dependence.

In the instance of the 7-8 profile type patients, it would appear that social pain in the form of forced marriages and similar consequences frequently served to satisfy the need for "sexual pain dependence."

Rado points out the difficulty of discriminating between schizophrenia and obsessional behavior in borderline cases. He states that the schizotype has two, genetically determined, impairments: (1) diminished pleasure capacity, and (2) distorted body awareness. In psychiatric practice, obsessional behavior must be distinguished from schizophrenia by the absence of "minute schizophrenic traits" and by an emotional resonance.

Rado also notes that, like conversion hysteria, classical cases of obsessional behavior are becoming rare because cultural styles have changed from attitudes of prohibitiveness to permissiveness in the education of children.

The findings for the 7-8 profile type are similar to those for Halbower's (1955) 8-7 group except that, with the slight variations in profile introduced by his contingencies, treatment prognosis was poor while in the present 7-8 profile type prognosis for psychotherapy or a few electroshock therapy treatments was more favorable. Hathaway and Meehl's (1951a) group of 7-8 cases included many neurotic obsessive-compulsive diagnoses but also included a variety of psychotic diagnoses.

8-1-2-3 (7-4-6-0) TYPE

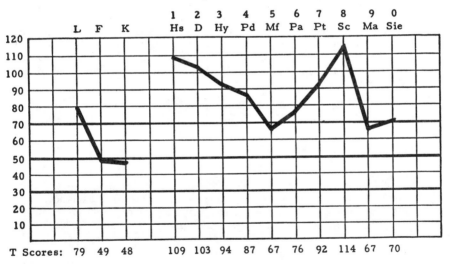

T Scores: 79 49 48   109 103 94 87 67 76 92 114 67 70

Rules

1. Hs, D, and Sc greater than T-score 80
2. Hs > D > Hy
3. Sc greater than Pt
4. F less than T-score 85
5. L may be greater than T-score 70
6. IQ may be below average

Mean Profile (N=6)

Diagnosis

Schizophrenic reaction, simple type.

Alternative Diagnoses

Paranoid or chronic undifferentiated schizophrenia; anxiety reaction in a schizoid personality.

Complaints, Traits, and Symptoms

Inadequacy feelings	(Blunted, inappropriate affect)
Hostile	(Dependent)
Poor work adjustment	(Tension)
Schizoid	

Cardinal Features

Extreme inadequacy in all life areas. Borderline somatic delusions, confused thinking. Flat affect. Usually single. If married, very inadequate adjustment. Withdrawn. Nomadic. Float from one job to another.

DISCUSSION

The markedly highly elevated profile with a primary elevation on Scale 8 would suggest a schizophrenic reaction. The APA *Diagnostic Manual* describes schizophrenic reaction as follows (p. 26):

> This term is synonymous with the formerly used term dementia praecox. It represents a group of psychotic reactions characterized by fundamental disturbances in reality relationships and concept formations, with affective, behavioral, and intellectual disturbances in varying degrees and mixtures. The disorders are marked by strong tendency to retreat from reality, by emotional disharmony, unpredictable disturbances in stream of thought, regressive behavior, and in some, by a tendency to "deterioration." The predominant symptomatology will be the determining factor in classifying such patients into types.

Although an occasional patient with the 8-1-2-3 profile type showed evidence of acute emotional disturbance, the usual picture was of inadequate affect and motivation suggestive of simple schizophrenia. The APA *Diagnostic Manual* describes schizophrenic reaction, simple type, as follows (p. 26):

> This type of reaction is characterized chiefly by reduction in external attachments and interests and by impoverishment of human relationships. It often involves adjustment on a lower psychobiological level of functioning, usually accompanied by apathy and indifference but rarely by conspicuous delusions or hallucinations. The simple type of schizophrenic reaction characteristically manifests an increase in the severity of symptoms over long periods, usually with apparent mental deterioration, in contrast to the schizoid personality, in which there is little if any change.

Family histories are sparsely covered in records of the 8-1-2-3 patients. Fathers are often described in terms such as "easy-going," and "big-hearted," while mothers are seen as nervous and unstable.

The 8-1-2-3 patients find short-term employment as laborers and float from one odd-job to another. More often than not, they are below average in intellectual performance, but even when test performance is better, achievement is very poor.

Almost always patients of this type remain single, but in the few instances in which they are married, the marital adjustment is also highly inadequate. They consider themselves to be, and usually are, sexually inadequate. These patients are socially withdrawn and aloof. Their outlook is a hostile, embittered one. They tend to lead nomadic existences.

Cameron (1944) has pointed out that although the official American classification of schizophrenia into Kraepelin's four types is convenient for descriptive and administrative purposes, the types rarely exist in pure form. Symptoms shift and categories overlap during the course of illness. He notes that the subgroups are much more clearly distinguishable early in illness, in acute episodes, or in cases that reach a stage of stabilization. If schizophrenia progresses to deterioration, the end product is highly similar regardless of the early picture. Cameron notes that this aspect led early classifiers to ascribe the illness to biological degeneration.

Writers such as Cameron (1944) and Henderson and Gillespie (1946) agree very closely in their descriptions of simple schizophrenia. These authors stress a gradual loss of interest beginning usually in adolescence. Onset is insidious and often perceived at first by those in the environment. Ambition is lacking. Shiftless lives with low level, constantly changing occupations and unemployment or asocial behavior patterns are the rule. Acute secondary schizophrenic symptoms such as delusions or hallucinations are usually lacking, but extreme apathy and emotional dulling are present.

The 8-1-2-3 profile type patients are characterized by extreme inadequacy in all areas of their lives. They come to the hospital with varied somatic complaints, sometimes of a borderline delusional nature. Although overt delusions and hallucinations are usually absent, thinking is confused and affect is flat. Inability to concentrate is usually reported.

There is a paucity of reported MMPI research relative to the 8-1-2-3 profile type. Guthrie (1949) found that peak 8 patients quite uniformly appeared to have been "borderline psychotics" with histories of short periods of confusion, disorientation, and a long history of vague somatic complaints which had been treated by a variety of regimens. Consistent with the present profile type, histories strongly suggested longstanding, stabilized, hypochondriacal trends.

(This profile type was developed from only six cases and was included partly to illustrate the kind of descriptions that could be developed for many other lower frequency profiles.)

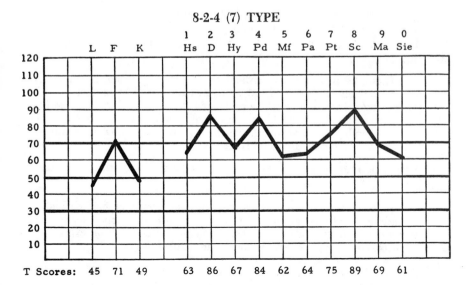

8-2-4 (7) TYPE

	1	2	3	4	5	6	7	8	9	0
L F K	Hs	D	Hy	Pd	Mf	Pa	Pt	Sc	Ma	Sie

T Scores: 45 71 49   63 86 67 84 62 64 75 89 69 61

Rules

1. D, Pd, and Sc greater than T-score 70
2. D or Sc greater than Pd
3. Sie less than T-score 70
4. Pa less than T-score 70
5. L and K less than T-score 70
6. Pd 10 or more T-scores greater than Hy
7. Sc not more than 13 T-scores greater than D

Mean Profile (N=9)

Diagnosis

Personality pattern disturbance, paranoid type.

Alternative Diagnosis

Schizophrenic reaction, paranoid type.

Complaints, Traits, and Symptoms

Immature	Restless
Inferiority feelings	(Anxiety)
Heavy drinking	(Depression)
Hostile	(Poor work adjustment)
Paranoid trends	

Cardinal Features

Extreme irritability, hostility, and tension. Single or, if married, severe marital maladjustment. Sexual psychopathology major problem. Oral, dependent, severe alcoholic. Lack drive and responsibility toward occupations. Guilt-ridden. Superficial acting-out.

DISCUSSION

With nearly equal elevations on Scale 4 and Scale 8, it is difficult to determine whether the emphasis is predominantly psychopathic or predominantly schizoid in this profile type, but a compromise seems to be offered by the diagnosis of paranoid personality.

The APA *Diagnostic Manual* describes personality pattern disturbance as follows (p. 35):

> These are more or less cardinal personality types, which can rarely if ever be altered in their inherent structures by any form of therapy. Their functioning may be improved by prolonged therapy, but basic change is seldom accomplished. In some, "constitutional" features are marked and obvious. The depth of the psychopathology here allows these individuals little room to maneuver under conditions of stress, except into actual psychosis.

The subgroup, paranoid personality, is further described as follows (p. 36):

> Such individuals are characterized by many traits of the schizoid personality, coupled with an exquisite sensitivity in interpersonal relations, and with a conspicuous tendency to utilize a projection mechanism, expressed by suspiciousness, envy, extreme jealousy and stubbornness.

Ewalt et al. (1957, p. 254) describe the paranoid personality category as follows:

> These people are usually somewhat like the schizoid personality but are less withdrawn, and are more rigid and better organized. They often have a great deal of energy and enter into external contacts in competitive activities. Through it all, however, they remain aloof, suspicious, and hostile. They keep the world at an emotional arm's length by biting sarcasm in verbal sorts of aggression and hostility. These persons, under great stress, may develop a full-blown paranoid psychosis. The psychopathology is the same as that mentioned for the paranoid reactions . . . but these people manage to keep their paranoid ideas at the level of suspiciousness, jealousies, and generally difficult natures.

Most outstanding in the backgrounds of the 8-2-4 profile type is a history of overly close, frequently seductive, interactions with mothers due to the absence of a father in the home as a result of causes such as death, divorce, illegitimacy, desertion and, frequently, the absence of siblings. There was often a history of poor school adjustment, with interpersonal difficulties and grade failures despite adequate intelligence. In some cases, there was a history of childhood sickness and resulting overindulgence by the mother.

Vocational maladjustment was frequent. These patients were lacking in drive, irresponsible, and occupationally very insecure. Aspiration for college and specialized training was frequently indicated, but there was not sufficient ego strength to complete these goals successfully. Modal occupation was bookkeeping or accounting. Strong feelings of failure were attached to vocational maladjustment.

The majority of these patients were single. When married, there was severe maladjustment. Deviant sexual orientation appeared to be a major problem. It appeared that the overly intensive relationship with mothers had resulted in sexual fantasies and guilt which arrested psychosexual development at a perverse level. Homosexual concerns, inordinate guilt about petting, overtly expressed incest concern, and bizarre sexual delusions in various patients all pointed to the depth of the sexual disorganization and guilt. Those individuals who were married carried on with other women, including prostitutes, to the dismay of their wives. The sexual difficulty in the marriages occurred in a context of extreme dependency and accompanying hostility toward wives.

Extreme irritability, hostility, and tension were common. Depression and insomnia accompanied these states of agitation. Severe alcoholism appeared to be symptomatic of strong regressive oral strivings in these hostile-dependent personalities. Many of these patients were concerned about the acting-out of other persons despite the fact that they frequently acted-out in similar ways with alcoholism and fighting. Although psychopathic acting-out was apparent on the surface, pervasive and apparently deep-seated guilt in conjunction with tendencies to deteriorate into frank psychosis over time indicated the malignancy of the underlying psychopathology.

In describing the "predominantly aggressive" type of psychopath, Henderson and Gillespie (1946, p. 386) state:

> Those who constitute this group exhibit disorder of conduct which may reach the highest degree of violence either directed toward themselves or

others. The characteristic feature is that it is not sustained but occurs in the form of episodes of shorter or longer duration, and is followed by a period of relative calmness, often with considerable insight into the occurrence. The attack, whatever the nature of it, seems to clear the air just as an epileptic fit so frequently does. The principal clinical feature of this group may be exhibited in the form of suicide, homicide, alcoholism and drug addiction, epilepsy, and sexual perversion. All of the above conditions may be part and parcel of an accompanying psychosis, but in the present instance we are considering them merely as features or symptoms of the underlying psychopathic state.

These comments would appear to apply very directly to the 8-4-2 profile type. They act out in psychopathic ways with alcoholism, hostility, and very often with sexual behavior that includes perversions and various deviations but, in time, they tend to deteriorate into frank psychosis.

Ewalt et al. (1956, p. 258) in their discussion of the antisocial reaction state:

> The impulsive and compelling character of these *psychopathic*[*] symptoms can be explained in several ways. Basically, the personal moral code or superego of these people is poorly developed. This is usually due to the fact that in infancy and childhood, when the patient was developing this facet of his personality, the environment offered unsatisfactory sources of love, security, and guidance. This might be due to a broken home, parents who reject him, or other environmental reactions which produced severe trauma when the child was in the early stages of his libidinal development.

These remarks would appear to be very pertinent in evaluating the background histories of the 8-4-2 profile type patients. In almost all of the cases, an overly close, possibly seductive, mother-child relationship could be inferred. Typical case history items were: father died when patient five; only child of mother's first marriage; never knew father; in children's home; lived alone with mother; father died of flu when patient was three; only child of widowed, neurotic mother; father suicided when patient six; mother treated like only child; alcoholic father salesman on road. Less inferential was one patient's statement, "I drink to have sex and then I am disgusted. I do to women what I wanted to do to my mother."

Ewalt et al. (1957, p. 259) also stated:

> Faulty or pathologic formation of the superego, which is the basic difficulty in the antisocial reactions, is felt to play a role in all the sociopathic disturbances. . . . The formation of a stable superego is dependent on several things. It is necessary for the child to have firm but dependable objects of love in his environment. These usually are the parents. The shifting of parents through a broken home, remarriage, parents who are too unstable or too cruel to function as a dependable source of love, or parents who behave in such a manner that the child cannot form proper standards of behavior through identification, may result in poor superego formation. If the parent fails to inspire love and affection in the child at about the fourth or fifth year, when the superego takes on definitive forms, the child will not react properly to the oedipal situation. The guilt feelings aroused by his changes in attitude toward his parents will not be great enough to arouse sufficient anxiety to stabilize the superego and enable the child to build one strong enough to influence his behavior in the future. If the child's first well-objectified hostility manifested in the oedipal situation is not toward a person loved enough

---

[*]Italicized word is ours.

to produce guilt feelings and strong anxieties, the pattern will be set for carrying out the gratification of the instinctual impulses without sufficiently strong guilt feelings or sufficiently strong fears of the consequences to cause a patient to inhibit or modify his behavior.

Ewalt et al. (1957) point out that deep study reveals that "psychopaths" are not free from remorse. "The restlessness, dissatisfaction, and continually moving from one love object to another in themselves offer a clue to the basic unhappiness." They note that this behavior has been described by Fenichel and others as running away from the superego.

In their discussions of sexual deviations, Ewalt et al. say that patients with sexual deviations are persons who have failed to develop beyond the infantile level of sexuality owing to arrested development or who have regressed to infantile forms of sexual expression. They attribute sexual deviations to the mechanisms of fixation and regression.

The severe alcoholism of the 8-4-2 profile type would also suggest fixation at an "oral" stage of development. Fenichel (1945, pp. 523-524) has described the formation of fixations on typical attitudes in the "oral character."

There appears to be little MMPI research directly relevant to this three digit code type.

8-6 (7-2) TYPE

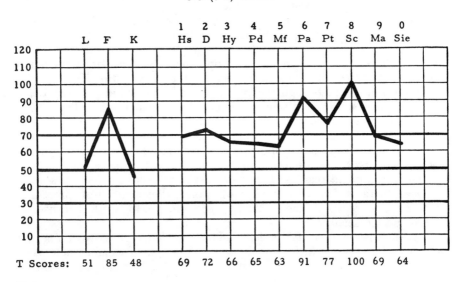

Rules

1. Sc and Pa greater than T-score 70
2. Sc and Pa greater than any other scales
3. F greater than T-score 70 does not invalidate profile

Mean Profile (N=10)

Diagnosis

Schizophrenic reaction, paranoid type.

Complaints, Traits, and Symptoms

Assaultive	Blunted, inappropriate affect
Auditory hallucinations	Suspicious
Bizarre paranoid delusions	Withdrawn, introversive

Cardinal Features

Florid schizophrenic thinking disturbance. Delusions, hallucinations, confusion, poor memory, and poor concentration. Shyness, withdrawal. Flat affect. Aggressive attacks may follow drinking. Usually single. If married, partner likely to be deviant. May have history of reasonably adequate ability to work but in period prior to onset of psychosis unable to function because of inefficiency and fatigue.

DISCUSSION

The high elevation of Scale 6 in addition to Scale 8 in the 8-6 profile type is consistent with the uniform diagnosis of the present sample as paranoid schizophrenics.

The APA *Diagnostic Manual* description of paranoid schizophrenia has already been given. (See page 42.)

A majority of patients in the 8-6 profile type were withdrawn, shy, and lacking in confidence and self-esteem from childhood. Backgrounds varied. Most frequent were broken homes due to death of a parent, desertion, or divorce. Less frequent were overprotective mothers. Overly dependent relationships as a means of deriving ego support from mothers, fathers, or siblings were frequently apparent. Some parents were described as detached. The exceptions in the uniformly poor histories of socialization were a few instances of successful participation in school athletics.

Failure to complete high school was most frequent but a few patients were good students in high school and one 8-6 patient was a college graduate. Skilled trades such as electrician were modal. Farm and factory laboring jobs were also frequent. One patient was a talented commercial artist who studied art after dropping out of high school. Histories frequently revealed apparently adequate vocational adjustment prior to military service but a failure to readjust following discharge from service. In several instances there was a history of good work adjustment. Just preceding hospitalization most of the patients were unable to work because of fatigue and inefficiency.

Seventy percent of the patients of this profile type were unmarried and showed a life-long history of shyness and failure to socialize heterosexually. When marriage occurred, spouses tended to be neurotic, alcoholic, and otherwise deviant.

The 8-6 profile type patients uniformly showed primary thinking disturbances characterized by confusion, poor memory, poor concentration, and forgetfulness as well as secondary, or accessory, symptoms of delusions and hallucinations. (Because of the apparent limiting effect of thinking disorders on IQ, the lower limit of 105 was not applied to this profile type.) Affect was usually described as flat. Withdrawal, shyness, and chronically unsatisfactory interpersonal relationships were usually described. On admission to the hospital, assaultiveness or threatened aggression were frequent, especially following heavy drinking.

There are many excellent reviews of schizophrenia in the literature such as the concise presentation in Ewalt et al. (1957). These authors state that schizophrenia comprises a group of reactions characterized by apathetic, silly, or unexpected emotional responses, by many varieties of defects in the thinking and associative processes and, in many cases, by the presence of delusional and hallucinatory phenomena.

No attempt will be made to duplicate the numerous exhaustive reviews of schizophrenia in the literature. There appears to be widespread agreement that thought disturbance is the cardinal symptom of schizophrenia. Writers such as Meehl (1962a) interpret the accumulated research as showing the basic defect in thinking, which Meehl terms "cognitive slippage," to be inherited but as indicating that the schizotype need not necessarily become clinically schizophrenic if environmental learning and support are highly favorable. In other words, the genetic abnormality of the schizotype is a necessary but not sufficient cause of clinical schizophrenia.

In some of the 8-6 cases, precipitating stresses were apparent. In the majority, however, it appeared that the patients had reached a phase in life where defenses and environmental supports were no longer adequate to prevent decompensation.

Most writers stress the greater ego strength of the paranoid type as compared to other types of schizophrenics. The work histories of the 8-6 profile type are consistent with this view, but with regard to prognosis, the 8-6 profile type patients tended to respond poorly to treatment such as electroshock and a majority had to be committed to neuropsychiatric hospitals for prolonged treatment.

Related 8-6 MMPI profile research has not been reported, but Hathaway and Meehl (1951a) found that most hospitalized patients obtaining 6-8 profiles were schizophrenics with paranoid delusions.

8-9 TYPE

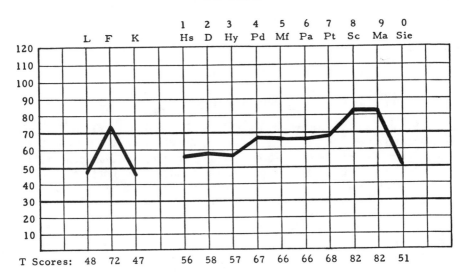

T Scores: 48 72 47   56 58 57 67 66 66 68 82 82 51

Rules

1. Sc and Ma greater than T-score 70
2. Sc and Ma greater than any other scales
3. Sc and Ma separated by not more than 15 T-scores

Mean Profile (N=9)

Diagnosis

Schizophrenic reaction, catatonic type.

Alternative Diagnoses

"Schizo-manic" psychosis; paranoid schizophrenia.

Complaints, Traits, and Symptoms

Circumstantial   Paranoid trends
Compulsive   Religious
Confusion   Restless
Father strict   Talkative
Financial status poor   Tension
Hostile   (Anxiety)
Hyperactive   (Depression)
Panic state   (Poor work adjustment)
Paranoid delusions

Cardinal Features

Hyperactive, unmanageable, tense, panicky. Vague and evasive. Disorganized thinking with hallucinations and delusions. Suspicious. Overtalkative. Excessive religiosity. High achievement needs but mediocre life performance. Transference proneness. May become indecisive, withdrawn, catatonic. If in excited phase, hostile, demanding, pacing, dazed, disoriented. Vocational indecision. Poor job role identification. Unhappy marriages. Occasionally married but usually single. Ambivalent. Poor sexual adjustment.

DISCUSSION

The high and almost equal elevations on Scales 8 and 9 of the 8-9 profile types suggest both schizophrenic and manic elements which could indicate either the more severe forms of manic-depressive, manic states or excited, elated schizophrenic states such as catatonic excitements. Patients in this profile type with one exception were diagnosed as schizophrenic reaction; case history data such as occasional instances of posturizing favor the schizophrenic diagnosis.

The APA *Diagnostic Manual* contains the category schizophrenic reaction, schizo-affective type, for patients showing "significant admixtures of schizophrenic and affective reactions" but states that this category is purely a descriptive one and points out that such patients usually prove to be basically schizophrenic. The *Diagnostic Manual* describes schizophrenic reaction, catatonic type, as follows (p. 26):

These reactions are characterized by conspicuous motor behavior, exhibiting either marked generalized inhibition (stupor, mutism, negativism and waxy flexibility) or excessive motor activity and excitement. The individual may regress to a state of vegetation.

In every 8-9 case, poor parental relationships prevailed. This was most uniformly the case in relation to fathers but resentment was frequently strong in relation to mothers and referred to their dominance and over-protectiveness. Relationships between parents were usually unfavorable with such manifestations as dissension, divorce, or separation. Poor relationships existed with siblings, who frequently appeared to represent parent surrogates. In a majority of cases, siblings were reported to be favored or more successful than the 8-9 patients.

The 8-9 profile type patients showed unusually strong achievement ideals despite histories of mediocre school and vocational achievement. Very strong sibling rivalry and marked frustration because of lack of success in actual strivings compared to siblings were frequently associated with the high achievement needs. Job histories revealed much vocational indecision and poor job role identification. Almost every 8-9 patient aspired to other than his actual vocation and to a much higher vocational level than he had achieved. These patients appeared to have much guilt associated with their failure to achieve at their desired level. Very strong avocational interests in outlets such as reading, music, or mechanics at times seemed to substitute for unattainable achievement needs. Unrealistic, compulsive needs for perfection were not attained partly because of lack of competence but partly because of hyperactivity, poor organization, and low frustration tolerance. Masculine aspirations and spatial aptitude seemed to explain the frequent choice of jobs such as carpenter, bricklayer, or other occupations requiring manual dexterity and spatial ability. The high activity level of the 8-9 patients frequently led to their holding more than one job at a time. Work adjustment was almost always made difficult by poor interpersonal skills.

Poor interpersonal relations also characterized marriages. No instance of a happy, successful marriage occurred in this group, in which only one-third of the sample were married in the first place. Ambivalence, poor sexual adjustment, and divorce were common. These patients reacted negatively to wives as mother substitutes who were domineering and pushing. Disorders in the interpersonal sphere were also reflected in a kind of "transference proneness" developed by several patients to therapists and to other hospital staff members. Occasionally, an attachment to an older woman was reported. These unrealistic emotional attachments frequently culminated in marked frustration and overreaction.

At the time of hospitalization, the 8-9 profile type patients were described as unmanageable, tense, and panicky. In addition to being hyperactive, they were vague and evasive, partly because thinking was primitive, disorganized, and disordered by delusions, hallucinations, and flight of ideas. Usually these patients were suspicious and overtalkative. In almost every case there were religious preoccupation and delusions of a type which indicated a searching for control from a powerful parental or father symbol. During the psychotic episode, some of these patients became very indecisive and withdrew to the point of catatonic immobility and posturizing. In most cases, excitement prevailed for some time and the patients were extremely hostile and demanding. They paced restlessly in a dazed, trance-like state in which they were disoriented and their behavior bizarre.

The 8-9 patients were usually given electroshock or insulin therapy but still required prolonged hospitalization. Even if there was favorable response to treatment, it was usually followed by a recurrence of the psychosis.

Arieti (1959 b, pp. 483-484) provides an enlightening discussion of the origins and functions of catatonic behavior. His discussion appears particularly relevant in light of the histories of the 8-9 patients. He states:

> People who are apt to become catatonic are those who in their early childhood have been prevented from developing confidence in their own actions and reliance on their capacity to will. The parents or parent substitutes have forced these patients either not to will or to follow parental decisions. When the patients later had to make their own choices, they found themselves unable to act; if they acted, they were criticized and made to feel guilty. In catatonia, the typical schizophrenic childhood struggle with significant adults is connected particularly with the actions and choices of the patient.
>
> The eventual catatonic may try to remove the anxiety which accompanies his actions by compliance or obsessive-compulsiveness. In precatatonic patients, in fact, we find strong ambivalent attitudes, pseudocompliance, and compulsions. But if the symptoms are not sufficient to protect the patient from excessive anxiety, or if they cannot be built up rapidly enough to dam the anxiety, catatonia develops. Catatonia is a removal of action in order to remove the panic connected with the willed action. Sometimes this panic is generalized. When it is extended to every action, the patient may lapse into a state of complete immobility (stupor). . . .
>
> At times the catatonic loses this inhibiting guilt-fear complex and acts in an opposite way—that is, as if he were not concerned at all with responsibility or as if he were defying previous feelings of fear of responsibility. His behavior manifests a manic-like sequence of aimless acts. He may become violent and homicidal. This is the state of *catatonic excitement.*

Previous MMPI research with 8-9 codes is sparse. Hathaway and Meehl (1951a) indicated that psychiatric patients obtaining profiles coded 9-8 showed a more malignant picture than patients with 9-4 codes. Guthrie (1949) found that medical patients with 9-8 codes and histories of hyperactive behavior sought medical help when depressions were imminent, but he did not find schizoid features in the 9-8 code type.

9 TYPE

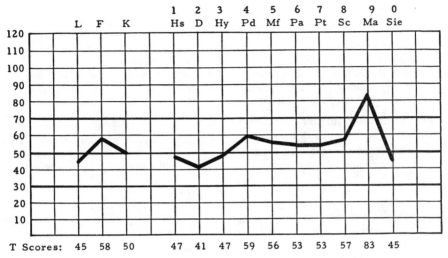

| | | | | 1 | 2 | 3 | 4 | 5 | 6 | 7 | 8 | 9 | 0 |
| | L | F | K | Hs | D | Hy | Pd | Mf | Pa | Pt | Sc | Ma | Sie |

T Scores: 45 58 50   47 41 47 59 56 53 53 57 83 45

Rules

1. Ma greater than T-score 70
2. No other scales over T-score 70
3. D less than T-score 50

Mean Profile (N=10)

Diagnosis

Manic-depressive reaction, manic type.

Complaints, Traits, and Symptoms

Circumstantial

Religious

Financial status poor

Talkative

Grandiose delusions

(Depression)

Hostile

(Heavy drinking)

Hyperactive

(Poor work adjustment)

Mother domineering

Cardinal Features

Hyperactive, grandiose, talkative. Previous attacks of depression or mania. Some evidence of genetic defect. Prone to "anniversary reactions." Overactive, many projects. During acute phase, thought and speech bizarre. Flare up with belligerency when crossed. Fear being slowed down because they can anticipate depression. Frequently married to wives of different religion. Turn to religion strongly during acute phase for control but at same time resent controls. Normal job adjustment and generally normal life adjustment between illness phases.

DISCUSSION

The high elevation on Scale 9 in the 9 profile type indicates a hypomanic state.

The APA *Diagnostic Manual* describes manic-depressive reactions as follows (p. 25):

> These groups comprise the psychotic reactions which fundamentally are marked by severe mood swings, and a tendency to remission and recurrence. Various accessory symptoms such as illusions, delusions, and hallucinations may be added to the fundamental affective alteration.
> Manic depressive reaction is synonymous with the term manic depressive psychosis. The reaction will be further classified into the appropriate one of the following types: manic, depressed, or other.

The manual further describes the manic type as follows:

> This group is characterized by elation or irritability, with overtalkativeness, flight of ideas, and increased motor activity. Transitory, often momentary, episodes of depression may occur, but will not change the classification from the manic type of reaction.

There are comparatively few broken homes in the backgrounds of the 9 patients. The most striking and consistent background finding appears to point to genetic or constitutional factors in that various parents, siblings, or relatives tended to be emotionally unstable, mentally ill, or hypomanic. Family stability in childhood was sufficiently good so that only one case appeared to show major character defects. Mothers, and occasionally fathers, were described as domineering, but this may have been because these patients elicited strong parental controls as a result of their childhood manifestations of hyperactivity. Resentment of earlier parental domination was frequently expressed. This resentment may have related to frustration over the imposition of controls by parents. (The resentment of controls is also manifested in adult life and was clearly apparent in the hospital situation.) In several cases, parents apparently reacted negatively to the child's personality; in some instances, mothers warned the patients in childhood that they could not tolerate the strain on their health of the patient's style of behavior.

Educational attainment appeared to vary within normal limits. Several patients were professionals such as a dentist and an engineer. A few failed to finish high school. Several were salesmen. The modal patient showed good job adjustment when not ill but some shifted from job to job, apparently because of hypomanic tendencies. Aside from the direct effects of hypomanic phases, job adjustment appeared generally to be normal.

In most instances marriages were stable and varied within normal limits. An unusually high frequency of instances in which patients married wives of a different religion suggested, in view of other aspects of these patients, that they may have been frustrated about religious controls just as they were about parental controls with resulting ambivalence in religious identification. Some appeared to lean on religion as a source of strength and control. There appeared to be a greater-than-chance number of wives with multiple miscarriages and of children with constitutional defects or illness, again suggesting possible genetic defects.

Every 9 profile type patient was hyperactive, grandiose, and talkative. Usually these patients stopped sleeping and engaged in multiple projects and activities far into the night. Almost all had previous attacks of hypomania or depression. Some of these recurred at regular intervals and some appeared to be "anniversary reactions." Thinking and speech usually became bizarre during the acute hypomanic phase. Most of the patients flared up and became extremely belligerent when blocked or crossed in their activity. Frequently, patients feared being slowed down because they could anticipate a pending depression. In many patients there appeared to be an underlying obsessive-compulsive makeup, with behavior during non-illness phases being characterized by neatness, precision, and high standards. Preoccupation with cars in several patients seemed to indicate possible compensation for inadequacies in the sexual sphere or for the hypothetical "small penis complex" of manics.

Treatment by electroshock and chlorpromazine usually produced some improvement. Often when chlorpromazine was reduced or discontinued, the hypomanic state flared up anew. About one-third of the patients had to be committed for longer term treatment. Those who were discharged usually had subsequent episodes.

Many excellent reviews of manic-depressive psychoses have been published. Arieti (1959 b) provides an extensive bibliography. Arieti states that the symptoms of manic attack are (1) a change in mood, which is one of elation; (2) a disorder of thought processes, characterized by flight of ideas and happy content; and (3) an increased mobility. He adds that accessory bodily changes also occur.

Arieti describes hypomania as occurring in "extroverted" personalities who begin to show pep and good humor. They want to do a lot of things. Their verbal abilities are accentuated. They may increase activities to the point of poor judgment, being compelled by their inner excitability and their exalted mood. They often go on spending sprees with disastrous economic consequences. Their sexual activity is increased and their lack of control may have unfortunate consequences. Their excitability, richness of movements, and euphoric mood give a bizarre flavor to their behavior.

All these descriptive elements would appear to be characteristic of the 9 profile type.

Arieti's observation that the early childhood of the future manic-depressive has not been so traumatic as that of people who tend to become schizophrenics or even severe neurotics is consistent with the present findings for the 9 profile type.

Arieti attributes the strong feelings of patriotism, religiosity, and political loyalty of the premanic-depressive to a strong tendency to introject parental figures. Like other writers, he notes that at particular points of development the mothers of these patients make high demands on them. However, Arieti freely admits that the dynamics are not well understood at present. Several writers report observations that indicate strength emanates from mothers and that weakness tends more frequently to prevail in fathers. Arieti describes three personality types among manic depressives: (1) self-conscious, inner-directed, (2) dependent, and (3) superficially lively, active, hearty, and friendly, often escaping into actions or reality but remaining shallow and dissatisfied.

Arieti mentions several common factors precipitating manic-depressive psychotic reactions: (1) death of a person important to the patient; (2) realization on the part of the patient of the failure of an important interpersonal relationship (generally with the spouse); and (3) a severe disappointment in a relationship to an institution or work to which the patient had devoted his whole life.

Arieti notes that these factors may be reduced to a single cause: loss of a valued object (1959b, p. 436).

Most writers on manic-depressive psychosis agree in attributing importance to genetic factors, but also stress dynamics such as "flight into reality," or "triumphant reunion between ego and ego ideal." It seems generally agreed that manic attacks defend against depression.

Cohen et al. (1954), in their intensive study of 12 cases of manic-depressive psychosis, found that in every case families were set apart from the surrounding environment by being "different" due to minority group membership, economic reverses, or illness and alcoholism of parents. These authors claim that in every instance the family felt the social difference keenly and reacted to it with intense concern and efforts to compensate. They observe that in a number of cases the child who was later to develop a manic-depressive psychosis was selected as chief carrier of the burden of winning prestige for the family. The necessity for winning prestige was most frequently engendered by the mother who was usually the stronger and more adequate parent, but this was not invariably so. Usually the fathers were thought of as weak but lovable. Although many of the observations relative to early family environments by Cohen et al. are in agreement with findings for the 9 type, their heavy emphasis on environmental explanations of the dynamics could be countered with a hypothesis regarding the nuclear role of familial genetic defects.

MMPI studies uniformly find that individuals obtaining peak scores on Scale 9 are energetic, ebullient, and sociable, but there is a paucity of reported research on psychiatric patients with the 9 profile type.

PART THREE

Summary and Conclusions

Chapter 5

Summary and Conclusions

In the preceding sections, personality descriptions have been presented for 19 MMPI profile types. An attempt has been made to relate these types to the psychiatric diagnostic nomenclature, to some of the common theoretical formulations regarding psychiatric disorders, and to some of the most relevant research findings on the MMPI. Impetus for the study grew out of clinical experience and it is hoped that the book will have considerable utility in the clinical situation. The actuarial approach to the description of personality seems already to have demonstrated its promise. If this book serves one of its intended major functions as a handbook of actuarial personality description, it should bring further evidence of the efficacy of the actuarial approach. It is also hoped, however, that the book will function as more than a handbook for the clinician who faces the diagnostic task of understanding and describing the personalities of psychiatric patients and of arriving at recommendations for treatment. An attempt has been made throughout the book to present hypotheses that are open to further research investigation. In the pages that follow, additional hypotheses of this kind will be emphasized.

The data presented in this book are not conclusive and the attempted interpretation of them has proceeded by gross matching and comparison (a) within the present data, (b) between the present data and empirical observations from other clinicians and (c) with speculative theoretical inferences from the present data and with inferences reported by other clinicians which also must be considered to have been speculative.

The homogeneity of the present sample is both a source of strength and a source of weakness for the generalizability of the data. On the one hand, there are inherent controls on extremely powerful variables such as test-taking set, sex, age, intelligence, and socioeconomic status in the present sample of veterans. These controls operate to make consistencies in theoretically important trait clusters more clearly apparent. On the other hand, when inferences are generalized to other populations, some shrinkage may occur.

There appear to be several source traits and environmental source factors that are of particular significance in determining the trait clusters associated with the various profile type groups. Autonomic nervous system overreactivity as associated most clearly with the 1-2-3 profile type would appear to be one such basic source variable. This finding is consistent with Murphy's (1962) conclusion from longitudinal studies of normal children that the autonomic reactivity is a basic determinant of "coping style."

The results of the present analysis show a consistent trend for high elevations on Hy (and the correlated elevation on Hs), as reflected most clearly in the 1-3-2 profile type, to be strongly associated with the environmental circumstance of childhood rejection and, in the male sample, particularly with rejection by father figures. Associated with this is a defect in masculine identification which parallels the characterological traits of repression, denial, and passivity.

Profile types with high Pt, as exemplified most clearly by the 2-7 profile type, show anxious temperament as a main determinant. Parents appear to exert strong influence in teaching standards and in inculcating achievement motivation to a degree which, at times, might be construed as overtraining. The strong parental influence appears also to yield strong positive identification, leading in the sample of males to firm masculine identification, to a capacity for emotional responsivity, and to the formation of deep emotional ties. These traits are in striking contrast to the deficiencies in such traits shown by the Hy and Pd profile types.

In the Pd profile types, as seen most clearly in the 4-9 type, active or aggressive temperament appears to be a trait of great significance. The environmental contingencies of most importance would appear to be predominantly maternal overindulgence or "spoiling" and predominantly paternal deficiencies in providing authority and control.

Thus far, the interpretations of the present profile types show similarities to tripartite typologies such as those of Sheldon (1942) and of Freud (1950). The 1-3 profile type would correspond to the viscerotonic, the 4-9 profile type to the somatotonic, and the 2-7 profile type to the cerebrotonic types of Sheldon and similarly to the erotic, narcissistic, and obsessional types, respectively, of Freud. The fact that neither Freud nor Sheldon included a schizophrenic or manic-depressive type implies that they perceived disjunction to exist between the varieties of normal personality and these psychotic deviations.

The working assumption which emanates from an over-all integration of the present data is that for most, and perhaps all, extreme personality deviations or psychiatric syndromes, genetic potential or aptitude is a necessary but not sufficient cause for the development of one type of deviation rather than another. As a corollary, it is assumed that for some personality deviations genetic potential is of primary significance. The data from the present study of the Scale 8 profile types would support the theories of Rado (1956) and Meehl (1962 a), who posit the presence of a genetically determined schizotypal personality as a necessary antecedent for the development of schizophrenia. The cognitive defects and defective pleasure ability (of which shyness or introversion may be one major consequence) mentioned by these writers is apparent in profile types such as the 8-6. Clear-cut environmental determinants are not apparent, but the data are most consistent with the view that the phenotypic expression of schizophrenia is influenced by such factors as the dynamics of early familial interaction. In addition, in the acute cases of schizophrenia among the 8-6 profile type patients, there is a suggestion that the typical florid reaction, frequently precipitated by an apparent low threshold for physiological effects of fatigue, infection, or toxins, often has at least surface similarity to certain types of organic psychoses.

The high Ma profile types, such as the 9, would appear to be associated with a defect related to the activation dimension. The concept of manic-depressive psychosis, as well as the present case history data, would suggest that the basic regulatory defect in activation leads both to extremes of depression and to extremes of mania. The findings of the present study agree closely with other studies regarding environmental consistencies in manic histories of families who are set apart socially because of differences from the prevailing culture but who provide sufficiently adequate support so that major character defects are not developed. These findings could be explained without resort to genetics, but the most parsimonious explanation would appear to be that a genetic defect leads to hyperactivity in the poten-tial manic patient, resulting in a characteristic reaction by the typical mother. This interaction takes place in a family in which other behavioral abnormalities exist among family members, frequently among fathers, which are also genetically influenced, although possibly phenotypically different and of diverse kinds.

Mixed types are apparent among the cookbook profile types. The main variables, however, appear to be the 1-2-3 autonomic instability, 1-3 repres-sion, denial and passivity, 2-7 anxiety, 4-9 aggressiveness and immaturity, 8 cognitive and affective defects, and 9 activation regulation defects. The mixed types quite clearly show the combined effects of these basic vari-ables. Thus, the 1-2-3-7 profile type is both overreactive in autonomic ner-vous system functions and anxious, the 1-3-7 type has the "hysteroid" trait cluster but is also anxious, the 1-3-8 type has "hysteroid" elements but is schizophrenic, the 9-8 type is both manic and schizophrenic, and so. forth.

Unsuccessful attempts to find a depressive profile type in sufficient numbers to serve as a cookbook type suggests that the D scale in at least one of its factors is measuring a state dimension which cuts across many profile types. Similar difficulty would be expected in efforts to specify a pro-file type that reflects anxiety as a state dimension and also paranoid agita-tion as a state dimension. It is the opinion of the present authors, based on research related to galvanic skin reactivity, that psychophysiologic tech-niques may eventually provide more precise measures of clinical states than can be obtained from psychometric techniques.

Some general implications for treatment are suggested by the present study. It would appear that there should be optimal, specific therapeutic measures that will be maximally effective for each profile type. If such measures can be identified, they should be catalogued and consistently applied to the treatment of each of the profile types.

General principles of psychotherapy such as those supplied by Rogers (1957) imply that a nondirective therapeutic interpersonal relationship can unlock behavioral potentials. Such principles may be most applicable to individuals within somewhat narrow ranges of personality deviation. For most of the more extreme deviates represented in the profile types, and in psychiatric syndromes, principles of therapy such as the Rogerian tech-niques frequently prove to be ineffective. The amelioration of acute states of distress by techniques such as drug treatment or specialized therapeutic techniques, environmental manipulation, and the use of interpersonal therapeutic support are frequently indicated. It would seem that these measures could be optimally tailored to each type. In addition, it would seem that accurate knowledge by the therapist of what the patient really is like in differential typological terms and the communication of this directly or by implication to the patient in the framework of a therapeutic relationship may be a desirable, if not a necessary, aspect of effective therapy with most of the patients included in the present profile types.

Whatever variety of psychotherapy or whatever combination of possible therapeutic techniques is deemed to be the treatment of choice, it would seem that therapeutic goals must be realistically determined by attention to the intertypal differences in response repertoires and in potentials for behavioral change that are differentially apparent in the profile types.

References

Aichhorn, A.: *Wayward Youth*. New York, The Viking Press, Inc., 1935.

Alexander, F., and French, T. M. (ed.): *Studies in Psychosomatic Medicine*. New York, The Ronald Press Co., 1948.

Allport, G. W.: *Pattern and Growth in Personality*. New York, Holt, Rinehart & Winston, 1961.

Arieti, S.: Schizophrenia. In Arieti, S. (ed.): *American Handbook of Psychiatry*. Vol. II. New York, Basic Books, Inc., 1959a, pp. 455-484.

Arieti, S.: Manic-depressive psychosis. In Arieti, S. (ed.): *American Handbook of Psychiatry*. Vol. II. New York, Basic Books, Inc., 1959b, pp. 419-454.

Cameron, N.: The functional psychoses. In Hunt, J. Mc V. (ed.): *Personality and the Behavior Disorders*. Vol. II. New York, The Ronald Press Co., 1944, pp. 861-921.

Cantor, J. M.: Syndromes found in a psychiatric population selected for certain MMPI code endings. Unpublished doctoral dissertation. Minneapolis, University of Minnesota, 1952.

Cattell, R. B.: *Description and Measurement of Personality*. Yonkers, N.Y., World Book Co., 1946.

Chodoff, P., and Lyons, H.: Hysteria, the hysterical personality, and "hysterical" conversion. *Am. J. Psychiat., 114:* 734-740, 1958.

Cleckley, H.: *The Mask of Sanity*. St. Louis, The C. V. Mosby Co., 1955.

Cobb, S.: *Emotions and Clinical Medicine*. New York, W. W. Norton & Co., Inc., 1950.

Cohen, M. B., Baker, G., Cohen, R. A., Fromm-Reichmann, F., and Weigert, E. V.: An intensive study of twelve cases of manic-depressive psychosis. *Psychiatry, 17:* 103-137, 1954.

Committee on Nomenclature and Statistics of the American Psychiatric Association: *Diagnostic and Statistical Manual, Mental Disorders*. Washington, D.C., American Psychiatric Association, 1952.

Dahlstrom, W. G., and Welsh, G. S.: *An MMPI Handbook*. Minneapolis, University of Minnesota Press, 1960.

Ewalt, J. R., Strecker, E. A., and Ebaugh, F. G.: *Practical Clinical Psychiatry*. 8th ed. New York, McGraw-Hill Book Co., 1957.

Federn, P.: *Ego Psychology and the Psychoses*. New York, Basic Books, Inc., 1952.

Fenichel, O.: *The Psychoanalytic Theory of Neurosis*. New York, W. W. Norton & Co., Inc., 1945.

Freud, S.: Libidinal types. In Strachey, J. (ed.): *Collected Papers*. Vol. V. London, Hogarth Press, Ltd., 1950. (Originally published in 1931.)

Freyhan, F. A.: Psychopathic personalities. In Christian, H. A. (ed.): *The Oxford Medicine*. Vol. VII. New York, Oxford University Press, 1955, pp. 239-256.

Friedman, S. H.: Psychometric effects of frontal and parietal lobe brain damage. Unpublished doctoral dissertation. Minneapolis, University of Minnesota, 1950.

Gilberstadt, H.: An exploratory investigation of the Hathaway-Meehl method of MMPI profile analysis with psychiatric clinical data. Unpublished doctoral dissertation. Minneapolis, University of Minnesota, 1952.

Gilberstadt, H.: A modal MMPI profile type in neurodermatitis. *Psychosom. Med., 24:* 471-476, 1962.

Gilberstadt, H., and Duker, J. D.: Case history correlates of three MMPI profile types. *J. Consult. Psychol., 24:* 361-367, 1960.

Gottesman, I. I.: Heritability of personality: a demonstration. *Psychol. Monogr., 77* (No. 9) (Whole No. 572), 1963.

Guthrie, G. M.: A study of personality characteristics associated with the disorders encountered by an internist. Unpublished doctoral dissertation. Minneapolis, University of Minnesota, 1949.

Halbower, C. C.: A comparison ot actuarial vs. clinical prediction to classes discriminated by MMPI. Unpublished doctoral dissertation. Minneapolis, University of Minnesota, 1955.

Hathaway, S. R.: Problems of personality assessment. Paper presented at XIV International Congress of Applied Psychology, Copenhagen, Denmark, August, 1961. *Proceedings of the XIV International Congress of Applied Psychology.* Vol. II. Copenhagen, Einar Munksgaard Forlag, 1962, pp. 144-160.

Hathaway, S. R., and McKinley, J. C.: *The Minnesota Multiphasic Personality Inventory Manual.* Revised. New York, The Psychological Corporation, 1951.

Hathaway, S. R., and Meehl, P. E.: The MMPI. In *Military Clinical Psychology.* Department of the Army Technical Manual, TM 8-242; Department of the Air Force Manual, AFM 160-45, 1951a, pp. 71-111.

Hathaway, S. R., and Meehl, P. E.: *An Atlas for the Clinical Use of the MMPI.* Minneapolis, University of Minnesota Press, 1951b.

Hathaway, S. R., and Monachesi, E. D.: *Analyzing and Predicting Juvenile Delinquency with the MMPI.* Minneapolis, University of Minnesota Press, 1953.

Henderson, D. K., and Gillespie, R. D.: *A Textbook of Psychiatry for Students and Practitioners.* 6th ed. New York, Oxford University Press, 1946.

Hoch, P., and Polatin, P.: Pseudoneurotic forms of schizophrenia. *Psychiat. Quart., 23:* 248-276, 1949.

Jenkins, R. L.: The psychopathic or antisocial personality. *J. Nerv. & Ment. Dis., 131:* 318-334, 1960.

Johnson, A. M., Falstein, E., Szurek, S. A., and Svendson, M.: School phobia. *Amer. J. Orthopsychiat., 11:* 702-711, 1941.

Kahn, E.: *Psychopathic Personalities.* New Haven, Yale University Press, 1931.

Kempf, E. J.: The conflicting, conditioned, self-determining attitude-basic mechanism of neurosis. In Gantt, W. H. (ed.) *Physiological Bases of Psychiatry.* Springfield, Ill., Charles C Thomas, 1958, pp. 127-170.

Lawshech, C. H., and Baker, P. C.: Three aids in the evaluation of the significance of the difference between two percentages. *Educ. Psychol. Measmt., 10:* 263-270, 1950.

Loevinger, J. Objective tests as instruments of psychological theory. *Psychol. Rep., 3:* 635-694, 1957.

Marks, P. A., and Seeman, W.: *The Actuarial Description of Abnormal Personality.* Baltimore, The Williams & Wilkins Co., 1963.

Maslow, A. H., and Mittelmann, B.: *Principles of Abnormal Psychology.* New York, Harper & Brothers, 1941.

McCord, W., and McCord, J.: *Psychopathy and Delinquency.* New York, Grune & Stratton, Inc., 1956.

Meehl, P. E.: *Research Results for Counselors.* St. Paul, Minn., State Department of Education, 1951.

Meehl, P. E.: *Clinical vs. Statistical Prediction.* Minneapolis, University of Minnesota Press, 1954.

Meehl, P. E.: Wanted—a good cookbook. *Am. Psychologist, 11:* 263-272, 1956.

Meehl, P. E.: Schizotaxia, schizotypy, schizophrenia. *Am. Psychologist, 17:* 827-838. 1962a.

Meehl, P. E.: Psychopathology and purpose. In *The Future of Psychiatry.* New York, Grune & Stratton, 1962b, pp. 61-69.

Meehl, P. E., and Dahlstrom, W. G.: Objective configural rules for discriminating psychotic from neurotic MMPI profiles. *J. Consult. Psychol., 24:* 375-387, 1960.

Mello, N. K., and Guthrie, G. M.: MMPI profiles and behavior in counseling. *J. Counsel. Psychol., 5:* 125-129, 1958.

Murphy, L.: *Widening World of Childhood.* New York, Basic Books, Inc., 1962.

Peterson, D. R.: Predicting hospitalization of psychiatric outpatients. *J. Abnorm. & Social Psychol., 49:* 260-265, 1954.

Preu, P. W.: The concept of psychopathic personality. In Hunt, J. McV. (ed.): *Personality and the Behavior Disorders.* Vol. II. New York, The Ronald Press Co., 1944, pp. 922-937.

Rado, S.: *Psychoanalysis of Behavior: Collected Papers.* New York, Grune & Stratton, 1956.

Rado, S.: Obsessive behavior. In Arieti, S. (ed.): *American Handbook of Psychiatry.* Vol. II. New York, Basic Books, Inc., 1959, pp. 324-344.

Rogers, C. R.: The necessary and sufficient conditions of therapeutic personality change. *J. Consult. Psychol.*, *21*: 95-103, 1957.

Rosen, A.: Development of some new MMPI scales for differentiation of psychiatric syndromes within an abnormal population. Unpublished doctoral dissertation. Minneapolis, University of Minnesota, 1952.

Sheldon, W. H., and Stevens, S. S.: *The Varieties of Temperament*. New York, Harper & Brothers, 1942.

Sullivan, P. L., and Welsh, G. S.: A technique for objective configural analysis of MMPI profiles. *J. Consult. Psychol.*, *16*: 383-388, 1952.

Sutherland, E. H., Schroeder, H. G., and Tordella, C. L.: Personality traits and the alcoholic: a critique of existing studies. *Quart. J. Stud. Alcohol*, *11*: 547-561, 1950.

Symposium: Automation technics in personality assessment. *Proc. Staff Meet. Mayo Clinic*, *37*: 61-82, 1962.

Weiner, H., Thaler, M., Reiser, M. F., and Mirsky, I. A.: Etiology of duodenal ulcer: I. Relation of specific psychological characteristics to rate of gastric secretion (serum pepsinogen). *Psychosom. Med.*, *19*: 1-10, 1957.

Weiss, E., and English, O. S.: *Psychosomatic Medicine*. 3rd ed. Philadelphia, W. B. Saunders Co., 1957.

Welsh, G. S., and Dahlstrom, W. G.: *Basic Readings on the MMPI in Psychology and Medicine*. Minneapolis, University of Minnesota Press, 1956.

Wolff, H. G., Wolf, S. G., and Hare, L. C. (ed.): *Life Stress and Bodily Disease*. Baltimore, The Williams & Wilkins Co., Inc., 1950.

Young, K.: *Personality and Problems of Adjustment*. New York, Appleton-Century-Crofts, Inc., 1947.

Zilboorg, G.: Ambulatory schizophrenia. *Psychiatry*, *4*: 149-155, 1941.

Zubin, J.: Socio-biological types and methods of their isolation. *Psychiatry*, *1*: 237-247, 1938.

Appendixes

APPENDIX I. *Percentage Frequencies of Check-List Items for General Abnormal Sample and Each Profile Type*

	General Abnormal	1 2 3	1 2 3 4	1 2 3 7	1 3 2	1 3 7	1 3 8	1 3 9	2 7	2 7 4	2 7 8	4	4 3	4 9	7 8	8 1 2 3	8 2 4	8	8 6	8 9	9	10
N	100	11	36	11	36	19	12	9	9	13	22	17	17	17	10	9	6	9	9	10	9	10
Abdominal pain	2	45**			18			33**														
Acting-out	5		11												22			11		11		30
Agitated	14				17			44*										11				
Anorexia, nausea, vomiting	7	45**	47**	36*	26*	42**	33*		38*	15	18	29	18	40	44	33			11	10		20
Anxiety	33	55	44	82**	53	67*	44		85*	56*	46		35						56	10		10
Apprehension	5	10													11							
Arm and hand pain	0		31**			11	22						53**	29**		17		11	11	30*	11	10
Assaultive	4					11			11				12	10		17		11	11	40**	22	10
Auditory hallucinations	4					11										33		11		10		10
Back pain	5	36**		36**	32**	22	33*		14	11	14		12	10	22	33						
Blindness, eye complaint	3			16												50						
Blunted, inappropriate affect	18				11	33			41*					10	11		11	11		60**	33	10
Cardiac complaint	3					11									11					10		
Check writer, embezzler	0			26**	17										22							
Chest pain	3	17*				11	15									17			20		33*	60**
Circumstantial	4														11							
Combative when drunk	5	10				33*		23				12								33*		10
Compulsive	6						11		14										11			
Conflict with girlfriend	14						67*	15		56*			20	60						11		30
Conflict with parent	11												20							11		
Conflict with sibling	30	18	53*	11	11	33		15	14	30	14	41	53		11	33	22		10	33	11	30
Conflict with wife	11		0			33										33			30	56**	33	30
Confusion (nonorganic)	2						22					24	12			17				10		
Constipation	7	10	11	11	11				14		14			10	11			20		20	22	
Crying, tearfulness	0								18	30	18	29	18	30	11	50						
Daydreams	19	27	33	73**	42*	42		23							22							
Dependent	1																					
Depersonalization																						

* Difference significant at .05 level.   ** Difference significant at .01 level.

APPENDIX I. Percentage Frequencies of Check-List Items for General Abnormal Sample and Each Profile Type—Continued

Item	General Abnormal	123	234	237	132	137	138	139	27	274	278	4	43	49	78	8123	824	86	89	9
Depression	43	45	58	64	32	75*	67	33	85*	52	87*	59	53	30	89	33	56	40	67	70
Diarrhea	4						11								11	17			8	
Difficult concentration	2							22			28*				33*			10	11	
Difficulty in walking	3															17				
Difficulty with co-workers	1			11									12	10			11		11	20
Disoriented	4					17												10	22	20
Disturbed by relatives	9				11															
Divorced or separated	12	64**		9		25	11	33		15			6				11		33	10
Dizziness	6		31	18	21															
Dyspnea, respiratory complaint	8	27**				50**														
Ear complaints (buzz, click, ring)	1																11			
Elated	1																11			
Emotional instability	9											35*					22		11	
Epigastric complaints	17		11	18		58**	22	22								17	20	22		
Evasive, defensive	22		36*	45**	16	22	22			15	11	12	12	40			22		11	10
Exhibitionist, voyeur	2			16		17					18	18	41**	12						
Father alcoholic	9	10	14			33**	11								11		22	22	11	
Father deserted, left	2					11	22								11		11	11	22	
Father died before patient age 12	8																			
Father domineering	4					17		11					18				22			
Father mentally ill	2						22*		23								11		11	
Father passive, weak	4					17												10		
Father physically ill	4																	10		
Father poor supporter	0																			
Father punishing	1					33**	11				12	12		10		11			11	10
Father rejecting	2	10														22			22*	
Father religious	1																		22*	10

* Difference significant at .05 level.   ** Difference significant at .01 level.

APPENDIX I. Percentage Frequencies of Check-List Items for General Abnormal Sample and Each Profile Type—Continued

	General	Abnormal	1 2 3	1 2 3 4	1 2 3 7	1 3 3 2	1 3 7	1 3 8	1 3 9	2 7	2 7 4	2 7 8	4	4 3	4 9	7 8	8 1 2 3	8 2 4	8 6	8 9	9
Father strict	3	18				16	17	22				18	12	12	10	33*	33	33	10	33*	10
Fearful	10	10					42*	33	11			32*		12		11			20	22	
Feelings of hostility and homicidal preoccupation	17																				
Feeling of sex inadequacy	8							11	11					35				22			
Financial status poor	6	10	44*			16	58**	44*			26**	14	29*	35**	30*		17			44**	50**
Forgetfulness	0	10																	20		
Grandiose delusions	1	18						11									17	11	20		50*
Guilt	13	27	0	27				22	56**	15	26	18			10	11		22	20		10
Headache	12	64**	22	36	21		17	22		30	7	18	41*	35*	10	33	33	22			
Heavy drinking	32	10	78**	18	37**	11	42**	56			96**		65*	76**	70*	22		67*	30		50
Heavy drugs					11		33								10						
Homosexual trends	1																			11	
Hostile	10	18	53*	27	21	21	42*	33	67**	23	15		24	35*	90**	11	50*	44*	10	44*	40*
Hyperactive	3																			56**	80**
Hypertension	2	18					17								10						
Ideas of reference and persecution	11					11															
Immature	17	28	28		11			11	11	23	30	32*	41*	35	10		17	22	30	11	30
Impulsive	6					36*		11			11	28		29*	20			36*		11	20
Inadequacy feelings	8		18					11	11	23		37**			20	22	50*	11	10	11	10
Indecision	3							11	22	30		23**				11	17		10	11	10
Inferiority feelings	5		27	18	26	11	42**		56**	23	30*	37**	18	12	20	44*	17	33		11	10
Insomnia	11	36*	34**	18	42*		17		22					29		11	17	33			30
Irritable	11	45*	42*		11		42**	22		46**	26	14	35		40*	22		33		22	30
Leg or knee pain	8	17	17			18															
Loss of consciousness	6	27			11		17		44*			23	18				17	11			
Loss of interest	2							11						18	10	11		22		11	10
Married	58	100	53	91	95	75	75	78	56	100	41	14	88	76	30	56	17		30	33	70

* Difference significant at .05 level. ** Difference significant at .01 level.

APPENDIX I. Percentage Frequencies of Check-List Items for General Abnormal Sample and Each Profile Type—Continued

	General Abnormal	1234	1237	132	137	138	139	27	274	278	4	43	49	78	8123	824	86	89	9
Moodiness	2	18				11					12	24**	10		17	11	10		20
Mother complaining	1																		10
Mother died before patient age 12	6	10			17												10		10
Mother domineering	3	14**				11	11				12					11			30*
Mother mentally ill	3		11			11													10
Mother nervous	4	18	14		17			11		14	24				33	11			
Mother overprotective	6		11								12		20			11		11	
Mother physically ill	4								14	14	12					11		11	
Mother punitive	4																	11	
Mother rejecting	0													11				11	
Mother strict	0					11								11				11	10
Neck pains and throat complaints	3		11					15				12							
Nervousness	30	64*	53*	73**	83**	44	56	69*	48	37	29	41	30	56	17	11	20	44	
Nightmares	2			32	17					14				11	17			11	
Numbness	6	27	36*			33*	33*			18					17			11	
Obsessions	1							30**											
Other pain	4					11											10	44	
Panic state	0														17				
Paranoid delusions (bizarre)	10			22		22							10		17		90**	44*	
Paranoid trends	10			11		11				14		12	20		33	44*	10	44*	10
Paresthesia, itching	2	45**	32*		33*	11								11					
Passive	8	18								18			10		17			11	
Perspiration	7	10					11									11			
Poor work adjustment (vocational maladjustment)	44	67*	36	0	44	44	22	23	45	37	53	35	70	56	100**	67	40	67	60
Quiet	0									18			10				10		

* Difference significant at .05 level.   ** Difference significant at .01 level.

APPENDIX I. *Percentage Frequencies of Check-List Items for General Abnormal Sample and Each Profile Type—Continued*

Check-List Item	General Abnormal	1 2 3	1 2 3 4	1 2 3 7	1 3 2	1 3 7	1 3 8	1 3 9	2 7	2 7 4	2 7 8	4	4 3	4 9	7 8	8 1 2 3	8 2 4	8 6	8 9	9
Religious	1						33*	11											33	
Religious conflict	3																	10	78**	30**
Restless	13	18	14						23			29	18	20	11		44*	10	44*	20
Retarded	3				22													10	11	10
Ruminations	1															17				
Schizoid	8				15											50*	11		11	
Sexual difficulty	0	27**					11	22								33	22		33	
Somatic delusions	3															17				
Speech difficulty	3															17		10		
Suicidal preoccupations	12	22		18			44*	11		11	23	18	24	50	22		33	50**	11	
Suicide attempt	6	20*					11	11		15			41**	20	22		11	10	11	
Suspicious	9	31**		17			33						18	20		17	33	30	33	30
Talkative	3							33								50	22	20	56*	70**
Tension	21	39*		75**			22	33	69*	52*	41	24	18	50	56*		22	30	33	30
Tremor and trembling	14	14		33			22	44*		26	14	29	12	20	11		22	20		
Ulcer	0	16		17			11		0	7						17	11			
Unmarried	30											82				50	67	70	20	
Unworthiness feeling	3								38*		32*		12				11		20	
Visual hallucinations	1															17				
Weak, tired, fatigued	9	10	27	37*					23		14		12						20	
Weight loss	6								15		14									
Wife pregnant or postpregnant	5																			
Withdrawn, introversive	16	11	20						18								44	10	44	10
Worrying	9	55**	20	36*	21		11	11	46*	19	51**	18	12		44*	17	11			

* Difference significant at .05 level.   ** Difference significant at .01 level.

Appendix II. Case Studies

Typical Case 1-2-3 Profile Type

Age: 33
Marital status: Married
Children: 2
Occupation: Tailor

Presenting Complaint

This patient was admitted with somatic complaints of several months' duration. Included were complaints of severe tickling pain in the thighs, similar pains of progressive severity in the arms, occasional pain in the head and neck, occasional itching, occasional nausea and emesis with anorexia occurring at any time of the day, and a steady dull ache in the epigastrium. Other complaints were occasional blurred vision, insomnia, muscle weakness, and headaches.

The patient had been admitted to the hospital four years previously with the same symptoms, plus irritability, weight loss, and a marked cancer phobia. His fear that he might have gastric carcinoma had been intensified by the death of a close friend from this illness. The patient's two older brothers have been hospitalized with similar complaints. Since the number "3" was of special significance to the patient, he felt that he would possibly be the next in his family to take on the family nervous complaints. On the earlier admission, it had been reported that everything annoyed the patient. He avoided seeing people and seemed to be off in a world by himself. He was moody and often he did not seem to hear when someone talked to him. He kept his feelings to himself and seemed not to want sympathy from anyone.

At the time of the second admission, the patient's wife reported that his condition had worsened. He had gotten along rather well until a year previous to this admission when his personality had changed markedly. He began to worry about everything. He came to feel that his friends were talking about him and that the world was against him. He was afraid to go into public places. Although he had been a champion golfer in his town, he now refused to play golf. He wanted all the shades in the house pulled down day and night. He became argumentative. He had been violent toward his wife who had become fearful of him. According to his wife, he would never indulge in any relaxation and there was never any laughter in the home.

About a month prior to the present admission, the patient's former employer died. This death was very upsetting to the patient. This employer had always taken a fatherly interest in him. At about the same time, the patient's father was diagnosed as having gastric carcinoma. He died while the patient was in the hospital.

Background Information

The patient was the third oldest in a family of three girls and four boys. Two of his brothers had suffered from mental illness. The patient was described as being closest to his oldest sister who was reported to treat him him as if she were his mother.

The patient was reared in a very strictly religious family. Both his parents were immigrants. The father was a laborer who was described as a very conservative man who could be quite stern at times. He was also described as being very ambitious and had held two jobs most of the time. The patient regarded himself as similar to his father in this respect. According to the patient, his father was a "wonderful person" who was understanding but not too happy.

The patient's mother, who was in her seventies at the time of the patient's second admission to the hospital, had always been a very hard worker and was unable to let down even in old age. She was a very strict Catholic. She was described as stern, not loving, old-fashioned, and not believing in modern ways. The patient's parents had been separated for nine years before the father's death.

Social Adjustment

The patient and his wife dated for four years before their marriage. Their two children were wanted babies. The patient and his wife relied on the rhythm method of birth control. Sometimes they went for several months without engaging in sexual relations. His illness resulted in no change in their sex life. Neither the patient nor his wife was described as affectionate.

Because they were having financial difficulty, the wife went to work about a year before the patient's first hospital admission. They bought a house and the wife wanted to help pay for it.

Course in Hospital

During his first admission, the patient was described as very defensive in interview. He felt that he was completely disabled physically and that his trouble was on a physical basis. Hospital staff felt that he was a quite hysteroid, hypochondriacal person, with somatization and some depression, who was repressing most of his conflicts. He was treated with insulin, carbon dioxide therapy, and electroshock therapy. Electroshock was the last method employed and the only one which seemed to offer relief. The depression lifted after 13 treatments. The patient was discharged in good condition with good prognosis.

At the time of the second admission, the patient displayed marked anxiety with mild depression and generalized somatization. His affect was somewhat peculiar in that he maintained a smile at all times and seemed to want to impress the psychiatrist with his superior abilities and his knowledge of medicine. Physical examination was essentially negative except for a chronic skin inflammation. Psychiatric and psychological examinations showed him to be an extremely dependent, passively aggressive, passively hostile, immature individual with some obsessive-compulsive characteristics.

During his second admission, the patient received some medication, but was treated mainly with psychotherapy. He showed marked improvement.

Typical Case 1-2-3-4 Profile Type

Age: 38
Marital status: Divorced
Children: 3
Occupation: Asbestos insulator

Presenting Complaint

This patient was first admitted to the hospital with complaints of tremulousness and inability to eat and sleep for the previous two months. He had been drinking excessively over a long period of time.

Six months after being discharged from the hospital for the first time, he was readmitted with complaints of depression, gastrointestinal discomfort, general nervousness, and worries. He had been drinking heavily for most of the six months and had lost weight. He had experienced severe headaches and weakness after he received a gash on his head. He spoke of feeling "blue" and wanting to "jump in the river." He had difficulty sleeping, poor appetite, and generalized retardation of speech and motor activity.

Background Information

The patient was the third of four children, having a brother eight years older than himself, a sister six years older, and a brother four years younger. The patient seemed to have related well to the older siblings but he showed hostility toward the younger brother who had achieved some degree of financial success. Both the older brother and sister had unsuccessful marriages which ended in divorce.

The patient continually described his mother as a domineering woman who tried to run the lives of her children. She was high strung and constantly sought medical attention. The patient said he rebelled at the age of 16 or 17 and asserted his independence. The patient also dropped out of school at this time after completing only 10½ grades. The patient said his mother continued to be domineering and interfering after all her children were married. She had very strong feelings against having her children drink.

The father was characterized as an easy-going person with whom the patient got along satisfactorily. He was employed as a carpenter. He died in his sleep about three years before the patient's entry into the hospital. The patient believed his father had heart trouble but there was also a history of cirrhosis of the liver although the patient denied that the father drank.

Social Adjustment

The patient had been employed for 15 years as an asbestos insulator. He belonged to the union. Although he had a history of frequent absences from work, he did not express any anxiety about being able to hold a job or find employment. He said he had been a supervisor of a crew of men but four years previously had decided "there was no point to the responsibility" and had requested a lesser job.

The patient married at the age of 24 after three or four months of courtship. At his report, his wife had no secure family ties and was a poor housekeeper and manager from the beginning. The patient said he taught her to keep house, but he complained that she placed too much responsibility on him for managing finances and for disciplining the children. Both the patient and his wife felt that the first few months of their marriage were their only happy times together. Quarreling began as soon as the first child arrived. The patient expressed considerable hostility toward the child. There were three children within five years, two girls and a boy. The patient showed some affection for the boy but only jealousy and hostility toward the girls. He said the older girl was unusually hard to get along with and identified her with his wife. The patient said he began staying away from home after work and drinking until he could come home to eat alone.

The patient was excessively jealous of his wife and often accused her of infidelity. He used abusive language to her and several times he had struck her. He was unusually jealous of the children. His wife reported that he was even jealous of the attention she gave the dog and cat.

There was a history of unsatisfactory sexual relations which the wife felt was probably her fault. She said the patient seemed never able to relate in a close manner to her.

The patient and his wife quarreled constantly. The patient maintained that "no woman was going to run him." He made excessive demands upon his wife such as insisting that she get out of bed in the middle of the night to cook unusual foods for him. He drank frequently, often until he had very little physical control. He was loud, aggressive, and hostile when drunk. Although he smashed cars and often hurt himself physically, he would fight anyone who tried to give him medical attention.

It was after one of the patient's drinking sprees that his wife separated from him and carried through on her plan to get a divorce. The patient subsequently had been living alone in a furnished room and was drinking most of the time. He felt that his depressed state was all his wife's fault and blamed members of her family and his mother. He had no insight into his own role in the situation.

Course in Hospital

Psychological examination showed the patient to be a dependent person of high average intelligence who demonstrated depression and anxiety. Psychiatric examination revealed tremors of the hands, lips, and tongue with slow speech and thinking. There were no ideas of reference, delusions, or hallucinations.

The patient was defensive and showed little motivation for psychotherapy even after several interviews. He was placed on drugs with a gradual reduction in anxiety and depression. The treatment was changed to carbon dioxide therapy with good results in a short time although the patient continued to drink on visits home. He refused referral to Alcoholics Anonymous. After about five weeks in the hospital, the patient was discharged, on his request, to return to work.

Six months after discharge, the patient returned to the hospital at his mother's insistence. After his discharge he had moved into his mother's home where he spent his time drinking and sleeping. He had continued to drink heavily and had not been able to work. He was placed in the work-house for nonsupport of his family. His symptoms upon readmission were depression, gastrointestinal complaints, generalized nervousness, and worries. He had severe headaches and weakness after suffering a gash on his head. He said he had thought of "jumping in the river."

Typical Case 1-2-3-7 Profile Type

Age: 47
Marital status: Single
Children: None
Occupation: Carpenter (retired)

Presenting Complaint

The patient was admitted to the hospital with the complaint of a constant dull ache in the epigastrium. This pain had become unbearably intense in the two days before admission.

The patient had been hospitalized at least 14 times over a 10-year period. In childhood and adolescence he had been healthy except for pleural pneumonia at age 20. His outward appearance on admission was one of a tall, robust, healthy individual. His first hospitalization occurred while he was in the Army when he was treated for sinusitis. He later received treatment in an Army hospital for an itch on both feet, sandfly fever, and later for another foot itch. He experienced his first feelings of nervousness and weakness when he first landed in the United States after the war. He was then hospitalized for pains in his neck, swollen neck glands, nervousness, headaches, a lung abscess (removed surgically) and abdominal pains. He continued for several years to complain of the abdominal pains. Each time no physical basis could be found for the pains. The patient then began to go from one hospital to another looking for a more satisfactory diagnosis. He traveled around to a number of cities and entered hospitals in each place. He even went to the Mayo Clinic. Regardless of the diagnosis or treatment, the symptoms remained.

Background Information

The patient was the tenth of eleven children. His parents were both over 40 when he was born. His father was a farmer whom the patient remembered as a thoughtful, good-hearted man with many friends. The patient stated that his father had not been very strict with the children. The father was found dead in bed of a heart attack at the age of 71. The patient was then 26 years old. His mother died the following year of diabetes and gallstones. The patient described his mother as good natured, nervous, and easily excited but as never irritable. He said she became easily frightened when the children were sick or hurt.

Since most of the patient's siblings were older than he, many of them were married and scattered around the country before he was grown. Three of them were deceased.

When the patient was 16 and in the seventh grade, he had dropped out of school to help his father on the farm. His school attendance had been irregular and he said that he had not been very interested in school.

Social Adjustment

The patient spent his youth as a farmer, but he had also worked as a carpenter for local contractors around his hometown. In the Army he had been a carpenter attached to a maintenance department of the engineer squadron. He liked army life. Although he was overseas for 30 months, he was never in combat. Upon his discharge from service, the patient worked as a carpenter, as a laborer for the highway department, and as a caretaker for the city dump. For the six years before hospital admission, however, he had been completely unable to work because of his health. Such tasks as mowing the lawn or putting up storm windows would so incapacitate him that he would be in bed for weeks afterward. He spent all his time lying on the couch watching television although he always dressed each day. He had had at least three girlfriends: a Turkish girl whom he was supposed to have married when she came to the United States but did not; an older widow who had been his landlady; and a divorcee with two children, ages 15 and 18, with whom he had been living in common-law union for two and a half years. He seemed to have established a mutually satisfying relationship with his common-law wife, but he had put off marrying her because of his health. He said he was not able to "take the responsibility of a wife and children." His family disapproved of the common-law union. The patient's pain usually subsided when he talked about his family's disapproval.

The patient lived on his disability compensation check while his girlfriend received ADC to support her children. The patient said he sometimes contributed something toward household expenses when there were financial problems. Both the patient and his girlfriend felt they got along well together. The girlfriend believed the patient confided in her. She thought that his only problems were his stomach pains and his headaches and that if he were free of those symptoms, he would have no further trouble. Because work aggravated the condition, she shielded him from doing any tasks around the house. She waited on him and gave him a great deal of attention. She felt the patient was sick and suffering. The couple had no social life, and the patient did not express any interest in anything other than watching television and driving cars, which he found relaxing.

When the patient became angry, he would express his hostility to his girlfriend by giving her a tongue-lashing or he would "blow off steam" when the children did something he did not like. She felt he was "irritable."

Course in Hospital

The patient had been in and out of many hospitals over a period of ten years. He complained of gastrointestinal pains, nervousness, tension, inability to sleep, pain in the back of the neck and chest pain, sore glands in the neck, headaches, sinusitis, restlessness, trembling, dizziness, a feeling that "everything was moving away from him," and a fear of falling. He drank heavily.

Physical examination was essentially negative. There were no abdominal findings. Psychological examinations showed a dependent person of low average intelligence who was functioning very inefficiently. He was strongly hysteroid with a great deal of emotional immaturity. Psychiatric examinations showed a passive, dependent person with symptoms of anxiety and tension who was preoccupied with his abdominal complaints. He was well oriented but somewhat defensive.

Over the years many methods of treatment had been tried, including electroshock and carbon dioxide inhalation. The patient was told his problems were simply nervousness, but he rejected any attempt at psychotherapy. Drugs were prescribed without any relief. Pentothal interviews and Desoxyn were not fruitful. The patient continued to complain regardless of treatment. The patient seemed to show a strong need for secondary gain and it seemed likely that he could become a chronic invalid. Staff felt the hospital had little to offer the patient. The prognosis was considered poor.

Typical Case 1-3-2 Profile Type

Age: 33
Marital status: Married
Children: 3
Occupation: Self-employed building contractor and carpenter

Presenting Complaint

The patient was admitted to the hospital with complaints of transient paralysis from the waist down, tingling of hands and feet, back pain, and feelings of nervous tension. He denied any fears or panic but described feeling that he wanted to cry.

The patient had had an appendectomy in service and blamed the spinal anesthetic as the source of all his back pain. He had been in several hospitals for the complaint of back pain. Each time the physical findings were negative and the diagnosis was "nerves."

Background Information

The patient was the youngest of six children in a family where there were drinking and poor morals. The patient felt closest to his next oldest brother. His parents were still living, but in the previous few years the patient had not been very close to his family.

The patient dropped out of school after completing the ninth grade. He had a chance to go to a vocational high school but he was not interested, he said, because he liked "to fight and go with girls too much." He once participated in a Golden Gloves tournament.

Social Adjustment

The patient was married at age 18 to a girl two years older than himself with a much better education and cultural background. He and his wife considered themselves happily married. They had three children. The wife felt the patient was a loving and good father who had many wonderful traits.

The patient had experienced a panic reaction when he was inducted into the army shortly after he was married. He said he was afraid his wife would not wait for him. While he was overseas, he became upset when he thought his wife was not saving the money he was sending home, but his wife was able to reassure him.

After discharge from the army, the patient used the money his wife had saved and built a house which he then sold. This transaction started their contracting business which has been successful. The wife ran the office and the patient took care of the construction. He was very dependent upon his wife to handle relations with his employees.

Even though the couple worked together, his wife felt the patient was too dependent upon her. During the month previous to hospitalization, the patient had refused to go to work and wanted to stay home with his wife. He had previously had temper outbursts, but his wife remained firm and set limits for him. Once he struck his wife and she threatened to leave him. He had never struck her again. They seldom quarreled.

Course in Hospital

Physical examination was essentially negative. Psychological examination showed a well developed, neat appearing male of high average intelligence. He did not show any particular impairment of function. He was superficially cooperative but appeared to be somewhat defensive and evasive. He lost control and wept several times during the interview, exclaiming, "They did something to my back in service . . . wish we could find it, would rather it be anything but nervous." During the psychiatric examination the patient was somewhat antagonistic at the beginning of the interview, but he cried intensely when asked, "What does your back condition really mean to you?" He was well oriented to time, place, and person but was preoccupied with his back condition. He said that the year before he had lost some of his drive. The psychiatrist noted that the patient was somewhat narcissistic. His judgment was fair, insight into his condition was poor, and his mood was somewhat anxious, but the patient usually exhibited *la belle indifférence*. Prognosis was regarded as poor, but outpatient psychotherapy was considered to offer a better prognosis than hospitalization.

Typical Case 1-3-7 Profile Type

Age: 30
Marital status: Married
Children: 3
Occupation: Salesman

Presenting Complaint

The patient was admitted to the hospital with complaints of knifelike pains through his head and body, gurgling and rumbling of the bowel, pain in the heart area, chills, diarrhea, muscle weakness in the neck, loss of equilibrium, and fears that he was suffering from bulbar polio or myasthenia gravis.

The patient had been manifesting symptoms over the previous year when he had closed out his electrical appliance business and changed to the job of a hospital supply salesman. At that time he had noticed a pain in his left flank, tightness in his chest, and sharp shooting pains in his back. He had seen several private physicians. While he had been on vacation six months previously, he had suffered a stiff neck, headache, and generalized aches and pains. He returned home fearing that he had polio, a brain tumor, or heart trouble. He had been unable to work more than one month out of the previous eight because of nervousness and physical symptoms which he was sure had an organic basis. Repeated physical examinations had not supported this conviction. When the symptoms continued, a private physician suggested that he enter the hospital for a complete examination.

Background Information

The patient was an only child. His parents were both over age 30 when he was born. His mother said she wanted more children, but her poor health kept her from bearing them. The patient characterized his mother as the dominant member of the family who wielded her power through recourse to illness and helplessness when frustrated in her desires. She suffered from gallbladder trouble and had experienced two nervous breakdowns. She was often hospitalized. The patient believed his mother was hypochondriacal and that he had inherited her nervousness. The father was described by the patient as a hard working, easygoing, steady person with a pleasant disposition. He was a toolmaker and provided well for his family. The patient indicated that he felt some resentment because his father allowed his mother to dominate him so. He encouraged his father to stand on his own feet but to no avail. The father also leaned on the patient.

The patient was married. He had two children and his wife was expecting a third child within three weeks after the patient's admission to the hospital. The patient appeared upset at the prospect of another child. The wife said all the children were wanted except this last child who was arriving before they could prepare for it financially.

The patient had been prone to illness as a child. He had had all the usual childhood diseases as well as chorea at the age of six, which was recurrent, and rheumatic fever at the age of ten. He had suffered most of his life from a spastic colon.

The patient felt he had too often had his own way as a child. He had never confided in his parents but preferred instead to work out his own problems. He cited many examples of how he had successfully thwarted his parents' authority.

The patient had been a good student who found schoolwork easy, although his teachers had thought him nervous. He had skipped one and a half grades but had failed several subjects as a senior in high school. He had to go to night school to complete work for his high school diploma. The patient said his school failure stemmed from loss of interest because he wanted to get a job. He wanted to be independent of his family.

After he left school, the patient engaged in numerous occupations. He had further training in vocational school in electricity and heat treating and as a tool and diemaker in the Navy. He had worked as a mechanic, a maintenance electrician, and a toolmaker. He owned a body shop and repaired wrecked cars. Even though he had been successful, he sold the shop after two years. He bought a store building and started an electrical appliance business but sold it after a year. He felt he did not have enough time for his family. He operated a small used car lot for a short while. He had become a salesman for hospital supplies shortly before his admission to the hospital. As a hobby, he collected and worked on antique automobiles.

Social Adjustment

The patient had a number of debts. He seemed to be living beyond his income. He requested financial help a number of times during hospitalization. As each problem was solved, he requested financial help for another problem. When he was told he could have no further financial assistance, he became hostile and vituperative. He insisted he was in emergent need of help even when shown other ways of handling his business affairs himself. The patient insisted that the Department of Veterans' Affairs pay his wife's hospital bill and became angry when this was not done.

The patient was not a sociable person. He preferred the companionship of his wife's family to outside acquaintances. He and his wife did not have many friends. He preferred working on his hobby of repairing automobiles to socializing.

The patient belonged to a rigid, fundamentalist religious sect. He was active in his church and taught Sunday School. He disapproved strongly of drinking.

Course in Hospital

Physical examinations were essentially negative. Psychological examination showed a cooperative, well oriented individual who spoke freely but was preoccupied with his physical symptoms. He carried a little book in which to write things he wanted to remember. He complained of poor memory, but tests indicated that he had good memory and superior intelligence. Psychiatric examination showed the patient to be suffering from mild anxiety and depression and preoccupied with his symptoms, which he insisted were organic. Although the symptoms were bizarre, there were no hallucinations, delusions, or ideas of reference. The patient was oriented and in good contact.

The patient resisted insight quite markedly. His symptoms did improve a great deal through talking about his problems. The day after his wife delivered her baby, the patient's symptoms returned temporarily. After a few days, however, the symptoms again subsided and the patient asked to be discharged to go to work. He planned to see a private psychiatrist on an outpatient basis. Staff believed that long term, outpatient therapy would be helpful, but regarded the prognosis as guarded.

Typical Case 1-3-8 Profile Type

Age: 32
Marital status: Married
Children: 4
Occupation: Machinist

Presenting Complaint

The patient was admitted to the hospital with bizarre delusions, emotional flatness, pains which he had been having for about a year, and sexual and marital incompatibility accompanied by sexual fantasies which began two months before admission.

The patient had been hospitalized previously. During the first hospitalization he was greatly preoccupied with sex and religion. He had a "vision" of not bringing up his sons right. He felt sexually stimulated by sermons in church. He thought his mind was moving too fast. He attributed great powers to the sun and commented that in winter people need more sex and sun. He was amnesic about many events. He drank heavily. He made bizarre sexual demands upon his wife and felt he was having troubles with his wife when she refused his demands. He read the Bible to his wife and felt that everything in the Bible referred to sex (e.g., Genesis meant "genitals", Pharisees meant "fairies").

The second hospitalization occurred five years later. All of the previous symptoms were present, but the patient was even less inhibited about his ideas. He had been drinking so excessively that he had a bloody emesis. He had tried to pick up women in bars, had tried to date his wife's friends, and had made repeated homosexual advances to the husband of a friend. He had suggested that his wife allow him to make sexual advances to his 12 year old son and on the day of his second hospitalization he had attempted a homosexual act with one of his sons.

Background Information

The patient was very defensive about his background. He was the sixth of seven children. His mother had died when he was eight years old and he had been brought up by his father, who was a strict disciplinarian. The youngest child was placed in an adoptive home after the mother's death. The patient's father had developed some preoccupations about religion for which he had been treated in a mental hospital.

The patient entered military service at age 17 and served as a radioman. He apparently made a satisfactory adjustment.

Social Adjustment

After the patient's return from military service he worked as a salesman and as a machinist. He had been regularly employed. He worked on both day and night shifts. As his illness progressed, he became depressed during the night shifts and frequently drank early in the morning on the way home.

The patient had been married for seven years and had had four children before his first hospitalization. The couple had had a normal social life, but as the patient became more ill, their social life became disordered because the patient often behaved in an uninhibited manner at parties and made sexual advances to both the wives and husbands of friends. The patient had become preoccupied with religion and depressed and withdrawn after talking with lay preachers on several occasions.

Course in Hospital

Physical examination was essentially negative. Psychological examination showed superior intelligence. Use of language was very idiosyncratic and thinking was bizarre but there was still some intactness of ego processes. During the psychiatric examination, the patient was well oriented but his affect was flat and he discussed his sexual problems and their presumed religious correlations with much vagueness and circumstantiality. Psychotherapy was attempted at first but was not effective. Drugs gave only minimal improvement. Eight electroshock treatments diminished sexual and religious obsessions temporarily. Although it was felt that improvement was superficial, the patient was allowed to return to work with the understanding that he could return to the hospital when necessary. Prognosis was judged to be poor and the patient subsequently had to be hospitalized for an extended period.

Typical Case 1-3-9 Profile Type

Age: 36
Marital status: Divorced—remarried
Children: Twins
Occupation: Electrician

Presenting Complaint

This patient was admitted to the hospital with extreme anxiety brought on by disturbance in his marital situation. He was afraid he might harm his wife or her boyfriend, especially if he started drinking, and he came to the hospital to seek protection for himself and to protect others.

The patient had been hospitalized eight years previously with many neurological symptoms. These included increasing double vision and blindness, deafness, headache, and paresis of the left side of the body. An exploratory craniotomy was done and the diagnosis of pinealoma was established. Since extirpation was not possible, deep x-ray therapy was instituted with marked decrease in symptoms. Frequent neurological checks subsequently had shown minimal residual except for increased anxiety and tension resulting in headaches, tremulousness, excessive perspiration and Raynaud-like phenomena involving the left side of the body. The headaches were dull but were acutely exacerbated by any anxiety-producing situation.

Background Information

Very little was known about the early family history of the patient. His father was not living at home, but whether he was deceased or absent because of marital conflict was not known. The mother was dependent upon the son for financial help although she ran a small seasonal business during the summer. The patient had one sister.

Social Adjustment

The patient was married and had twin sons. The couple had separated; when the wife became pregnant by another man, the patient divorced her. After about six years, the patient again established contact with his former wife and persuaded her to divorce her husband and to remarry him. After eleven days of being remarried, however, the wife left the patient during an argument, returned to her second husband, and sued for divorce. The patient, fearing he might harm his wife or her spouse while drinking, sought admission to the hospital.

The patient had attended one year of college until the symptoms of his brain tumor became too uncomfortable. He had a good work history as an electrician for a power plant.

Course in Hospital

Physical examination was essentially negative. No suicidal or homicidal content was noted on psychological examination. On psychiatric examination the patient was well oriented. Moderate agitation was noted. There was no hallucinatory or delusional thinking. Realistic planning was noted. Present status of brain tumor was unchanged.

On admission, the patient slept almost continuously for 24 hours after which his anxiety and depression seemed improved. He was discharged after a few days of hospitalization.

Typical Case 2-7(3) Profile Type

Age: 44
Marital status: Married
Children: 4
Occupation: Highway engineer

Presenting Complaint

The patient was admitted to the hospital with complaints of anxiety and depression which had grown progressively worse during the previous few years. The patient complained of numbness in the arms and legs, and he was restless, tense, and agitated. He also had a panic reaction to the thought of losing his job.

The patient had not been hospitalized previously.

Background Information

The patient was the second of six children. His father was an immigrant. There were financial problems all during the patient's childhood. He and his brothers had to go to work at an early age to contribute to family finances. The patient resented this. The patient described his father as a rather passive person and his mother as more dominant.

The patient had a high school education. Except for two years of Army service, he had been employed by the highway department for the previous 21 years. He had been very successful on his job and had been promoted several times until he was finally made a squad leader. The patient became panicky at the thought that he could not do the job well. He cited many things he did not know. He finally became too upset to go to work. He asked for a demotion and still remained afraid that he would not know how to handle the new job. The boss was very pleased with him and could not understand why the patient asked for a demotion. There was no realistic danger that the patient would lose his job.

Social Adjustment

The patient had been happily married for 17 years. There were four children. He was kind, gentle, and affectionate with his children. He had recently become irritable and restless, however. He was overly critical of his wife so that nothing she did suited him. He seldom complimented her. The wife took the passive role except when things were especially important to her. After the patient became ill, he adopted a very clinging attitude toward his wife, which she found difficult to accept. The patient read a great deal. He was argumentative with his friends, but had many and was sociable and enjoyed groups. The couple enjoyed dancing and playing bridge.

Course in Hospital

Except for slightly elevated blood pressure, physical examination findings were negative. The patient was extremely tense and depressed on psychiatric examination. He was oriented. There were no delusions or hallucinations. He expressed extreme concern over his job adjustment. This concern did not have a great deal of reality basis. He seemed obsessed with the problem and finally had to be forbidden to talk about it during interviews before progress could be made. The patient was seen for a number of interviews by the psychiatrist.

The patient was placed on tranquilizers, which allowed him to relax and to sleep better. Each time he tried to do anything realistic about his job, he returned to the hospital more fearful, agitated, and depressed. Six electroshock treatments were given with good results. The patient was discharged to return to work immediately rather than to ruminate further about it.

The prognosis was judged to be guarded.

Typical Case 2-7-4 Profile Type

Age: 25
Marital status: Single
Children: None
Occupation: Liquor salesman, tavern operator

Presenting Complaint

The presenting complaint was excessive drinking. The patient had recently been discharged AWOL from the Tuberculosis Service where he had been hospitalized for the previous year. On admission to the Psychiatry Service he was in good contact and stated that he wanted help in combating his alcoholism.

About six months following discharge from military service, the patient began to notice increasing loss of energy and easy fatigability. He was found on examination to have active tuberculosis and was hospitalized. There was no other significant medical history.

Background Information

The patient was the youngest of four children. His siblings, two brothers and a sister, had achieved well. His father was a retired lawyer who was described as being hard-driving himself and as setting high standards for his children. At his parents' insistence, the patient attended a small college for one year, but did not apply himself and did poorly.

The parents appeared to have little knowledge of the patient's drinking problem, but the patient revealed that he had been a heavy drinker since his junior high school year. He stated that very early he drank a case of beer per day. He claimed that at the peak of his drinking in Korea, he was consuming between two and three "fifths" of liquor per day.

His parents reported that as a child the patient always had a good disposition and was not a behavior problem. After discharge from service, however, he was hostile, critical, and resentful toward his parents, and accused them of trying to run his life for him.

Social Adjustment

The patient was unmarried but was reported to be courting a girl of "doubtful virtue" toward whom the patient's mother was very negative. He made his home with his parents after being discharged from military service, but they saw little of him because he spent most of his time in a tavern which he and a partner had been operating in a nearby town.

Course in Hospital

Physical examination showed the patient to be a short, well built, athletic young man in no distress. Laboratory tests were negative. Psychological examination showed superior intelligence. On psychiatric examination, the patient was well oriented. He appeared motivated to work on his alcohol problem. He described one episode of possible delirium tremens. He complained of chronic anxiety dating from childhood. Diagnoses were chronic anxiety reaction, with alcoholism, and chronic bilateral pulmonary tuberculosis.

Treatment was of a supportive, directive kind. The Tuberculosis Service followed the chest condition. Vocational guidance was obtained and rehabilitation recommended. Contact with Alcoholics Anonymous was strongly advised. Prognosis was rated as fair.

Typical Case 2-7-8 Profile Type

Age: 23
Marital status: Single
Children: None
Occupation: Student

Presenting Complaint

The patient complained of chronic depression which had lasted for about two years and which had been worse in recent months. He also complained that he had no close friends and felt unable to trust people. The patient had no previous hospital history of significance.

Background Information

The patient felt that his condition was definitely based on an unsatisfactory and unhappy childhood. He described his parents as strict, old-fashioned, rigid, and domineering. They did not believe in athletics, music, dancing, or any pleasures from social interaction or recreation. The patient felt that, as a result, he had no social graces and that he was completely inadequate and inferior in interpersonal relationships, especially with girls.

The patient's mother appeared to be eccentric and had many unusual ideas. She was a college graduate and had been a schoolteacher. According to the patient, his mother lacked spiritual values of any kind and ridiculed the concept of love. She came from a well-to-do family and felt that she had married beneath her station. The patient described her as a resentful and bitter woman who constantly deprecated her husband's family.

The patient's father had only a fifth grade education. He was described as being talented despite his meager schooling but as having never capitalized on his potential. He had been a farmer and carpenter. The father gave little financial support to the patient, who had earned his own expenses from early adolescence.

The patient was the third in a family of four children. He described his older brother as being very headstrong, stubborn, and opinionated. In childhood he had picked on the patient and had frequently ridiculed his puny size. The parents seemed to favor the patient least of the children. The patient's second oldest brother accepted the parents' values and seemed to be happy and well adjusted. The patient's younger sister was described as stubborn. During childhood he had squabbled with her a great deal and they had never gotten along with one another. The patient lost a year at school because of scarlet fever and, as a result, was in his sister's class. He surpassed her academically by a very small margin and became salutatorian of the class. During high school the patient attempted to date but became infatuated with every girl he dated. Each time, however, he had felt that his feelings were not reciprocated and had become disappointed. The patient felt that the absence of normal ability to relate heterosexually was one of his greatest problems.

Social Adjustment

The patient had been living with his second oldest brother and had been having little social activity. He had made abortive attempts to engage in activities such as athletics and dancing, but his only regular social activity had been to tag along to bars with a group of older fellows. He drank a little but mainly listened to the conversation taking place around him. During military service he became engaged to a girl who left him without returning his ring. He described her as moody and unstable. He was upset by the termination of this romance, but later felt that even if he had the opportunity, he would not marry her because the marriage would only lead to more unhappiness.

When the patient came to the hospital to seek help, he was contemplating entering the university to study law and still retained this hope. During military service, he had uneventful duty in the Air Force. His service was largely in Germany, which he tolerated but did not like.

Course in Hospital

On physical examination, the patient had drooping of the eyelids, but findings were otherwise negative. On psychological examination, the patient showed superior intelligence. He also showed sex confusion with an overlay of anxiety and depression. On psychiatric examination, the patient was agreeable, cooperative, voluble, neat, fluent, and somewhat anxious and depressed. He ruminated at length about background family relations. He expressed feelings of insecurity and inadequacy and was concerned about inability to get along interpersonally.

Intensive psychotherapy produced little improvement and increased intellectualization but insulin therapy seemed to facilitate some working through of homosexual conflicts, anxiety, and authority problems. At termination of treatment the patient enrolled in law school but it was felt that treatment had produced only some symptomatic relief.

Typical Case 4 Profile Type

Age: 33
Marital status: Married
Children: 3
Occupation: Spray painter

Presenting Complaint

The patient was admitted for suicidal threats and excessive use of alcohol. He was inebriated at the time he sought hospital admission and seemed extremely depressed.

The patient had been hospitalized previously for kidney stones and had been treated several times over a period of ten years in hospitals for alcoholics. He had attempted suicide several times by turning on the gas, but always in situations in which he could be rescued.

Background Information

The patient was the youngest of five children. He had three sisters and a brother. He was four years younger than his next oldest sibling and was babied a great deal at home. Discipline was quite permissive. He says that he did not learn respect for discipline or authority. The father was an alcoholic, but was a stable workman. He was abusive to the patient's mother. The patient's brother was also an alcoholic but had been able to stay dry for the previous five years. Both parents died of cancer, the mother when the patient was 14 and the father when the patient was 32. The patient had completed a vocational high school education. He had had a long history of erratic employment at a number of different semiskilled trades. The longest he had worked at one job was 18 months. He felt he changed jobs because of an inner discontent. He stated that he was unable to take any kind of pressure.

Social Adjustment

The patient had been married for 11 years and had three boys ages 10, 9, and 8. Most of his married life had been full of friction. His wife described him as being very dependent on her for all decision-making. When he drank, he became irritable and depressed and often threatened suicide. He was quarrelsome and aggressive and several times had beaten his wife and abused the children. He expressed guilt about his treatment of the children. He ran up excessive debts when drinking. There were many financial problems. The wife had to work to help to support the family. There had been several separations but no attempt at divorce. The wife said she felt sorry for her husband when he came "crying back to her." He had been both unfaithful and exceedingly jealous. To the children he often made promises he did not keep. The patient had never been able to talk over problems but acted impulsively and relied on his wife to straighten out results.

Course in Hospital

The patient was hospitalized for only about ten days after which he was discharged because of his realistic need to return to work. He had calmed down with drugs and bedrest. He was given very directive supportive psychotherapy. The staff felt that the patient was quite immature, and the prognosis was guarded.

Typical Case 4-3 Profile Type

Age: 37
Marital status: Married
Children: 2
Occupation: Unemployed machinist, interior decorator, instrument repairman

Presenting Complaint

Presenting complaints were headaches, blackout spells, swollen glands, and attacks of rage. During a rage reaction, the patient began to choke one of the children of his mistress and became frightened. He had a history of many episodes of choking his wife. His wife had ejected him from their home several months before the presenting episode.

The patient had one prior admission to the hospital. About two years after discharge from military service he had been admitted because of temper tantrums and poor emotional control, especially manifested in repeated attempts to choke his wife. During his first admission, he also was evaluated for bilateral chorioretinitis which was found to be inactive.

Background Information

The patient was the oldest of five children. He had difficulty in getting along with his next younger sister. The patient's mother was described as being improvident, given to tantrums, and a poor homemaker. The patient's father was a telephone lineman who was electrocuted at age 40 when the patient was 12. He had drunk somewhat to excess but otherwise had been adequate. The patient's mother was pregnant at the time of her husband's death and became bedridden for many months. She managed the insurance money so poorly that the family soon was in bad financial straits. The patient's mother displayed frequent bouts of anger toward the patient and he felt that he did not receive enough affection. The patient adjusted poorly to school. After a long history of learning difficulty, he finally quit school in the tenth grade to go to work. The patient helped family finances by turning his pay over to his mother. He held many jobs such as mechanic's helper and truck driver until he finally enlisted in the Army in 1941. He served overseas and had considerable combat. In 1944, he was hospitalized for battle fatigue and later for anxiety that was service connected.

Social Adjustment

The patient met his wife while on a military furlough. They were married after four months of acquaintance. When he returned from military service, the patient adjusted poorly both to marriage and to work. He was restless and dissatisfied. He preferred to go off with male friends and gave his wife little attention or affection. The patient's wife worked; when she returned from work in the evening, he was extremely demanding and dependent. The atmosphere at home was very tense and the patient could easily be precipitated into an outburst of temper which often resulted in choking. When the situation finally became intolerable to his wife, the patient agreed to her request that he go to the hospital.

By the time of the patient's second admission, there had been a long history of marital and vocational instability. The patient had separated from his wife and children and she had filed for divorce. He complained that his wife had been unappreciative and disinterested. He said that he still loved his children. Following the separation, however, the patient began to live with a divorcee and her three children and was rehospitalized when he attempted to choke one of her children.

Course in Hospital

The patient was well developed and well nourished. The physical examination was essentially within normal limits. The patient was of average intelligence. He showed little evidence of emotional discomfort. He was described as a passive-aggressive personality. On psychiatric examination, the patient was alert, hyperkinetic, pleasant, cooperative, and oriented. When he was first hospitalized, he had episodes of severe headaches.

The patient was placed on a small dose of a tranquilizer. He adjusted well in the hospital and showed no apparent distress. In psychotherapy, he related only superficially. His mental content during interviews mainly concerned his dissatisfaction with his marriage and the impending divorce. Prior to entry into the hospital, he had been working on a road construction job but had quit and failed to provide support money. He expected to be able to find work and was discharged after several weeks.

Typical Case 4-9 Profile Type

Age: 22
Marital status: Single
Children: None
Occupation: Used car salesman

Presenting Complaint

The patient was brought to the hospital under court order signed by his parents. He had been sitting home for a month watching television all day. He was chronically angry, refused to talk to his parents, and neglected his appearance.

There was no previous history of treatment or hospitalization.

Background Information

The patient was the middle child of three. He had an older sister and a younger brother. The patient described his mother as a dominating, unaffectionate, critical, controlling woman who whined and complained a good deal. His father was described as quiet, unassuming, meek, and stable. He was a cab driver. The patient's mother had high praise for the patient as a child. She had held great hopes for him. She had thought of him as being more mature than he actually was because he had always been physically larger than the other children. As a child, the patient began to have friction with his parents and resented their attempts to control him.

Social Adjustment

After the patient's return from military service, his mother was perplexed by his attitude and felt as if "there was a small volcano in him." He obtained a job selling used cars, but lost it after a short time. The patient got into one minor scrape after another. His parents and relatives bailed him out of these scrapes. His father got him a job driving a cab, but he had so many accidents that he was discharged after a short time. He lied frequently and had temper tantrums.

The patient was quite expansive and bragged about his ability as a salesman. He admitted to selling questionable products but seemed to suffer no guilt about this. He stated that "nobody honest really gets ahead in the world." The patient was very antagonistic toward his mother and very critical of his father. The patient had a girlfriend but they broke up after he treated her badly and quarreled with her.

Course in Hospital

The patient was a tall, well-built man. The physical examination was entirely negative. He appeared to be of average intelligence. There was no evidence of anxiety, depression, or other emotional distress on psychological tests. Test results indicated a sociopathic personality. On psychiatric examination, the patient was well oriented and his affect was appropriate. He was likeable during interviews. His story was markedly inconsistent with that of his parents. He expressed frank and outspoken resentment and anger toward his parents.

The patient was seen mainly for evaluation. He was referred for vocational counseling and an attempt was made to improve his relationship to his parents. Following discharge from the hospital, the patient drank, lied, showed very irresponsible behavior at home, and wrote bad checks to cover gambling debts.

Typical Case 7-8 Profile Type

Age: 37
Marital status: Married
Children: 3
Occupation: Store manager

Presenting Complaint

The patient came to the hospital with complaints of chest pain and depression. Two weeks earlier the patient had gone to his minister and confided in him that he was depressed and had suicidal ideas. The patient also complained of difficulty in concentrating and increasing nervous tension. The minister informed the patient's wife of his visit. When she broached it to the patient, he collapsed completely.

There had been no previous hospital admissions for emotional disturbances.

Background Information

The social worker obtained scant background history because the patient was uncommunicative and his wife was highly defensive, claiming to know little of the patient's background.

The patient came from a family of driving, ambitious people. He had three sisters and was the only boy in the family. As a young man he worked for his father in a retail store. All of his siblings were highly successful.

Social Adjustment

The patient had been manager of a unit in a large corporation. About a year before his hospital admission he had been transferred to a small division of the company and was disappointed at the outcome of the transfer. He returned to his former job but lost interest and became depressed.

His wife stated that the patient had always felt inferior and inadequate in all areas and was constantly anxious about his performance. He had strong preoccupations about not having achieved as well as he should have.

The patient attended college for a short time but contracted poliomyelitis and withdrew. He met his wife shortly after his illness and never returned to college. Three children were born in rapid succession, causing considerable marital stress. The patient served in the Navy and was exposed to combat during the war. After discharge he was thin, restless, and indecisive. He drank heavily to relieve tension.

The patient was very dependent on his wife. Their life contained little recreation or frivolity. There was a considerable overtone of incompatibility. His wife appeared to be an attractive, defensive, hostile, cold person.

Course in Hospital

On psychiatric examination, the patient complained of chest pains, inability to concentrate, feelings of failure and depression, and loss of interest. He admitted to suicidal thoughts. He was self-depreciatory and felt that his family would be better off without him. He ruminated about past mistakes and failures. Psychological examination showed high average intellectual capacity. There was no apparent loss of efficiency. Patient was described as bogged down, worried, ruminative and passive-dependent.

The patient was given electroshock and psychotherapy. He appeared to gain a better understanding of himself. He felt that this understanding would help him to avoid future emotional breakdowns. He seemed to respond particularly well to group psychotherapy and said that it helped him to realize that other persons had similar and even more serious problems than he had.

Typical Case 8-1-2-3 Profile Type

Age: 30
Marital status: Single
Children: None
Occupation: Clerical worker, factory worker, laborer, hospital attendant, etc.

Presenting Complaint

This patient was admitted with complaints of nervousness, feelings of isolation from other people, and social withdrawal. He felt that he was losing his grip. He disliked his frequent job changes and was perplexed and confused because he could not decide if he was in the right occupation.

He had many physical complaints. He perspired excessively when around other people, his eyes bothered him when he tried to read, he was bothered by constipation, and he was concerned about a wide variety of somatic symptoms.

Background Information

The patient was the oldest child in a family of two girls and three boys. All of his siblings were married except the second oldest who was still at home with his parents. The patient's father was the owner of a small construction company. He was described as an intelligent, easygoing, casual, big-hearted man who only worked when he had to. He was also described as being respected and well liked but superficial in his relationships with his family and his friends.

The patient's parents were never happy together. His mother was a nervous, irritable, energetic, excitable woman who worried a great deal. She suffered from gallbladder trouble and a heart condition. She wanted her first child to be a daughter and treated the patient like a girl for his first five years.

The patient attributed all of his difficulty to his "inadequate social background." He blamed both his parents and his teachers for this. He was always extremely shy and particularly unable to relate to girls. During his school days he was very sensitive about his severe acne and dissatisfied about his size—first, because he felt that he was too tall and, later, in the high school years, because he felt that he was undersized. His only feeling of self-satisfaction was in relation to his intelligence and academic ability. After high school the patient served in the Navy. He was socially withdrawn but liked the work of a pharmacist's mate because he felt that he was making use of his ability.

Social Adjustment

After discharge from military service, the patient attended an art school for a few months but quit because of feelings of tension. He entered a university but left before the first quarter final examinations. He enrolled in a second university but became tense and left after two quarters. He began to work at a series of jobs. He stayed at one job as a hospital attendant for a year but other jobs were only of a few months' duration. He felt that all of the jobs he tried were far below his capacity.

The patient spent little time in his hometown with his family but traveled around the country from place to place and job to job.

Course in Hospital

The patient showed very compulsive behavior. He insisted on writing a detailed history for the social worker so that there would not be any errors. He thought that if he had a tape recorder, he could record word definitions and increase his vocabulary. He felt that he had no social graces and no knowledge of sports, dancing, or girls so that he was unable to make friends or engage in casual conversation. He felt inadequate in most respects but different and superior to others intellectually. He felt that he was a puzzle to other people.

Physical examination was negative. Psychological examination showed very superior intelligence. Thinking was bizarre and autistic. Feelings of futility about the future were apparent. During psychiatric examination the patient showed obsessional thinking and paranoid attitudes. Psychotherapy was tried but found to be quite ineffective. The only positive response to the hospital was shown during art therapy. The staff considered the patient to be an ambulatory schizophrenic with a guarded prognosis at the time of discharge.

Typical Case 8-2-4 Profile Type

Age: 26
Marital status: Married
Children: 1
Occupation: Student

Presenting Complaint

The patient was brought to the hospital when he began to drink heavily in a local tavern and the bartender noticed that he was spending his money foolishly and was talking in a strange manner.

Since discharge from military service, the patient had been hospitalized twice previously for outbursts of rage and aggression following prolonged drinking sprees.

Background Information

The patient's father was an Army captain who died at the age of 40 when the patient was five years old. The father's death was caused by injuries sustained during the first World War. The patient's father was considered to be an outstanding man and the patient idealized his image.

The patient described his mother as a pleasant person. Following her husband's death, she went to work and entrusted the patient's care to her mother who became his primary mother-figure. The patient's mother remarried when he was eight years old. Within a short time she had a child from this marriage. These events were a great shock to the patient. Shortly after the birth of the child, a boy, the patient's mother obtained a divorce from her second husband. She returned to work and again left him to the care of his grandmother. The patient never became really familar with his stepfather. He disliked his half-brother and felt very hostile toward his mother after her second marriage.

The patient was a bright student and, during school years, was interested in athletics, reading, and Scouting. He was uncomfortable at home and sought as many outside activities as possible. He felt estranged from his mother and was unable to express his hostility toward her. The patient served in the Army for five years as an enlisted man. He spent several years overseas, but his service experiences were not unusual.

Social Adjustment

The patient's wife was in military service when they met. They married after two months of acquaintance. The wife very soon became pregnant. The couple were both eligible for discharge from service shortly after the marriage. The patient tried a number of clerical jobs. He began to do some drinking. When the wife returned to her parents during her confinement, the patient went to live with his mother. After the birth of the child, the patient visited periodically until finally the patient, his wife, and his child all moved in with his mother and half-brother in their small, one bedroom apartment. The patient and his wife were unable to find accommodations so continued living in the very crowded conditions. Matters came to a head when the patient, after having been gone all of one weekend on a drinking bout, came home in a very irritable state and created a great deal of disturbance. He threatened to kill a cab driver, broke furniture, and become so upset and hostile that his wife called the police. In court the judge advised the patient to seek help. He then went to the hospital, where he was admitted. The patient adjusted poorly after discharge from the hospital. He drank excessively, moved from job to job, and was generally unhappy. Finally, he decided to move with his wife and child away from his family and back to her home state to enter college. He had another episode of disturbed behavior, however, and was hospitalized for three months, during which time he was diagnosed schizophrenic reaction, paranoid type, and given deep insulin treatment. Following the treatment he adjusted well for a few months but then began to drink again and to behave irresponsibly. Eventually, the patient enrolled in the university and managed to do acceptable work and to hold down a parttime job for one quarter. After an episode of rage and fighting for which he was jailed, however, he was sent to a neuropsychiatric hospital where he was hospitalized for four months and received electroshock treatment. For the following eight months, he again attended the university until his wife became ill with poliomyelitis. He became depressed and disturbed and was rehospitalized. Over the succeeding years, he was hospitalized numerous times with the recurring picture of depression, rage reactions, suicide attempts, and alcoholism. His marital and occupational adjustment was maintained at a very marginal level.

Course in Hospital

Physical examination was essentially negative. The patient tested in the very superior range of intelligence and showed no loss of intellectual efficiency. He appeared to be depressed, paranoid, overideational, and impulsive. On psychiatric examination, the patient was relevant, coherent, and oriented. He denied delusions or hallucinations. He was well controlled and appeared to have recovered from what appeared to be an acute toxic state due to alcoholism.

The patient was able to pull himself together in the hospital and was released after a few days when he asked to leave because he was anxious to register at the university.

Typical Case 8-6 Profile Type

Age: 44
Marital status: Single
Children: None
Occupation: None

Presenting Complaint

The patient had drunk excessively and had become disturbed. He threatened neighbors and relatives and tried to choke his mother. The police were called and took him to jail, from which he was transferred to the hospital.

The patient previously had been diagnosed paranoid schizophrenia. He had been hospitalized twice at a neuropsychiatric hospital. During one of these admissions he had been treated with a long series of electroshock treatments.

Background Information

Sparse developmental history was obtained. The patient had attended grade school and high school. Prior to military service, he had been a carpenter's apprentice. During service he suffered from a psychotic break and subsequently had not been able to work. His mother was very defensive about the patient and tried to minimize the seriousness of his illness, attributing his recent behavioral disorder to drinking. She did blame herself for his difficulties and thought that perhaps she had babied him excessively. The patient's father was more realistic about the patient. He was concerned about his son's inability to work, his poor judgment in secretly buying an automobile, in driving without a license, and in buying guns which the father took away from him. The patient was resentful about the latter because he felt that people were plotting against him, particularly some Japanese individuals who, he thought, were masterminding the plot.

Social Adjustment

After discharge from his first postservice hospitalization, the patient complained of chronic fatigue and did little or no work. His only constructive activity revolved around raising rabbits and maintaining a rabbit hutch. He spent much of his time at the nearby family lake cottage where he lay around, listened to music, and drank beer. On several occasions he became hostile to neighborhood children who, he said, let his rabbits out of the hutch. He kept a gun and was reported by neighbors and police to have threatened his parents with a gun. He became particularly irritable when his demands for money to buy beer were refused. The patient had been on a trial visit from the neuropsychiatric hospital, but when his behavior became clearly dangerous, he was returned to the hospital after a court hearing.

Course in Hospital

The physical examination was essentially negative. On psychological tests, the patient appeared to have average intellectual capacity, but he was very inefficient in abstract reasoning in a manner which was consistent with a primary thinking disorder. Testing showed schizophrenic idiosyncratic thinking and grandiosity. At the time of psychiatric admission examination, the patient was very defensive and denying, but he did say in a somewhat bizarre way, "I don't have any stomach once in a while." His affect was flat but otherwise he was able to cover up. At the time of a prior admission, the patient had admitted to delusions of persecution. He thought that an organized group wanted to kill him to get his money and that his parents were a part of the group.

The patient was treated with chlorpromazine but showed little response to the drug.

Typical Case 8-9 Profile Type

Age: 32
Marital status: Married
Children: 4
Occupation: Student

Presenting Complaint

At a Christmas party, the patient had what was apparently a catatonic episode. He appeared to lose consciousness, stared into space, clenched his fists, and later cried uncontrollably and became violent. On arrival at the hospital, he experienced auditory and visual hallucinations. He claimed that he was getting help from the sun. He saw Christ and received messages from Him. This acute episode lasted for ten days.

Background Information

The patient's parents had an unhappy marriage. His mother had a boyfriend who spent a good deal of time around the home. The patient's father was away much of the time operating his small business. His parents separated when the patient was four and he was placed for five years with a paternal aunt. Following this, his parents reunited although his mother continued to maintain the relationship with the other man. According to the patient, his mother was very rejecting. She forced him to clean house and to do hard, menial household tasks rather than permitting him to play with other children. At times she completely ejected him from the house and then called the police to find him. When the patient's father died, his mother married the other man.

Social Adjustment

After finishing the ninth grade, the patient escaped from his unhappy home situation by entering military service. He had a very strong desire to excel and alienated people by his display of vocabulary. He completed high school after discharge from service and entered college where he hoped to study medicine. He found the courses difficult, however, and after obtaining a B.A., he entered a graduate course in library science.

The patient met his wife during his undergraduate college period. He converted to her religion and showed great zeal. While he was attending college, the couple had four children and suffered great financial stress. The patient worked at outside jobs and had to leave school for short periods to improve finances. The family had no recreational outlets and few friends. Shortly before his psychotic break the patient had been severely disappointed when his application for a professional job was turned down because of a poor recommendation based on an incidence of insubordination on an assembly line job during his college days.

Marital relationships were complicated by the wife's shyness and timidity and by traumatic pregnancies. Their religion prevented them from attempting birth control.

Course in Hospital

Physical examination was normal. On psychological tests the patient demonstrated superior intellectual capacity but showed some loss of intellectual efficiency. During testing he was defensive, hostile, pedantic, and intellectualizing. During psychiatric examination at the time of admission, the patient was actively hallucinating, hyperactive, and showed some clouding of consciousness. He thought that he and God were bombing the city. He was disoriented and bizarre in behavior.

The patient was placed on physiological therapy and psychotherapy. After 60 days of hospitalization, he was tried at home for a week. He became depressed and hallucinatory, however, and was rehospitalized. After another two months of hospitalization with tranquilizing medication and psychotherapy, he was discharged.

Typical Case 9 Profile Type

Age: 44
Marital status: Married
Children: 3
Occupation: Packing house worker and stationary engineer

Presenting Complaint

The patient was admitted to the hospital with symptoms of grandiose delusions, hyperactivity, and overtalkativeness of two months' duration. He had become preoccupied, indecisive, and inefficient at work.

The patient had had four previous hospital admissions for episodes either of depression or of hypomania. During depressions, he would become irritable with his family, guilty about not earning his salary, and generally preoccupied with feelings of unworthiness. During these attacks he would be uncommunicative and show severe psychomotor retardation. During hypomanic episodes, he would become hyperreligious and exceedingly overtalkative about his love for his family, job, church, and people in general. He would sleep little and engage in projects such as digging up pansies and transplanting them in his minister's yard at 3:00 A.M. At these times he would show restlessness, flight of ideas, and agitation.

Background Information

The patient's father was a bricklayer. He was described by the patient as a stern man who was too busy to spend much time with the patient during his childhood. He was also described as a moody man who was excitable and overtalkative. Several relatives had been treated for nervousness. The patient's mother was an exceedingly proud woman who warned the patient that if he ever caused embarrassment to his family, they would disown him. Both parents were extremely perfectionistic. They were very preoccupied with their own interests and were critical of their children. They were not members of an organized church, but they attended services at a church which believed in healing illness through faith. The patient was a middle child with two sisters. He had always considered himself to be a failure and worried about his parents' opinion of him. He felt hurt when he did something that he considered worthwhile and his parents showed no interest in his achievement. He had inner feelings of rebelliousness toward them but never acted openly upon them.

Social Adjustment

The patient married a girl of different religion, which very much upset his mother. He and his wife lived in a house owned by his wife's aunt. It was only a few blocks from her parents' house. The patient had some feelings of resentment about domination by his in-laws. He also resented interference by his parents.

The patient was a high school graduate. He had difficulty in the ninth grade but otherwise succeeded in high school.

The patient worked for the same packing house for many years and received several promotions. He suffered his first episode of depression shortly after discharge from military service and a second episode at the time of a job promotion.

TEXAS A&M UNIVERSITY - TEXARKANA

The patient and his wife had experienced a satisfactory marital relationship. They had three children, two of whom were born by cesarean section and the middle one of which, a girl, was mentally defective. The patient's greatest conflicts lay in the area of religion and in fears that he would be unsatisfactory in his work and fail to meet his high perfectionistic standards.

Course in Hospital

The physical examination was essentially negative. Psychological examination showed the patient to have superior intellectual capacity with no evidence of decreased efficiency. Test results reflected his euphoric, grandiose state and showed underlying anxiety and compulsiveness. On psychiatric examination, the patient showed euphoria, grandiosity, and press of speech. He was circumstantial, with flight of ideas and loose associations. He felt that he was having revelations of a sexual and religious nature. He had delusions of abnormal sexual potency.

The patient's delusions and euphoria gradually decreased with tranquilizing medication.